CRIMINAL JUSTICE, LAW ENFORCEMENT AND CORRECTIONS

INTERNATIONAL CRIMINAL COURT: DEVELOPMENTS AND U.S. POLICY

Criminal Justice, Law Enforcement and Corrections

Additional books in this series can be found on Nova's website under the Series tab.

Additional E-books in this series can be found on Nova's website under the E-books tab.

Global Political Studies

Additional books in this series can be found on Nova's website under the Series tab.

Additional E-books in this series can be found on Nova's website under the E-books tab.

CRIMINAL JUSTICE, LAW ENFORCEMENT AND CORRECTIONS

INTERNATIONAL CRIMINAL COURT: DEVELOPMENTS AND U.S. POLICY

MICHAEL N. BAKER
EDITOR

Nova Science Publishers, Inc.
New York

For permission to use material from this book please contact us:
Telephone 631-231-7269; Fax 631-231-8175
Web Site: http://www.novapublishers.com

NOTICE TO THE READER

Library of Congress Cataloging-in-Publication Data

International Criminal Court : developments and U.S. policy / editor, Michael N. Baker.
p. cm.
CRS report for Congress prepared for members and committees of Congress.
Includes bibliographical references and index.
ISBN 978-1-61324-694-8 (hardcover : alk. paper) 1. International Criminal Court. 2. International criminal courts--Political aspects. 3. United States--Foreign relations--21st century. I. Baker, Michael N.
KZ7312.I58 2011
345'.01--dc22

2011015365

Published by Nova Science Publishers, Inc. † New York

CONTENTS

PREFACE

The International Criminal Court (ICC) is the first permanent international court with jurisdiction to prosecute individuals for "the most serious crimes of concern to the international community." While the U.S. executive branch initially supported the idea of creating an international criminal court, the U.S. ultimately voted against the Statute of the ICC and informed the United Nations that the U.S. did not intend to become a State Party to the Rome Statute. The United States' primary objection to the treaty has been the potential for the ICC to assert jurisdiction over U.S. civilian policymakers and U.S. soldiers charged with "war crimes." This book focuses on the jurisdiction, extradition and U.S. policy of the International Criminal Court.

Chapter 1- The International Criminal Court (ICC, or Court) was established in 2002 as the first permanent court to prosecute war crimes, crimes against humanity, and genocide (together, "ICC crimes"). Pursuant to a provision in the Statute of the International Criminal Court ("Rome Statute" or "Statute"), the States Parties to the Rome Statute agreed to review the Court's activities seven years after its establishment. In compliance with this provision, the States Parties convened a Review Conference in Kampala, Uganda, May 31–June 11, 2010.

After declining to officially participate in the activities of the ICC or in the sessions of the Rome Statute's Assembly of States Parties (ASP) since the Court was established in 2002, the United States shifted its stance and began attending ASP meetings as an observer in November 2009, signaling a new policy of engagement with the ICC. At the Review Conference, the United States participated fully as an observer.

Chapter 2- The International Criminal Court (ICC) has, to date, opened cases exclusively in Sub-Saharan Africa. Twenty-two cases are currently before the ICC, all of them pertaining to crimes allegedly committed in five African states: Kenya, Sudan (Darfur), Uganda (the Lord's Resistance Army, LRA), the Democratic Republic of Congo, and the Central African Republic. The ICC Prosecutor has yet to secure any convictions. In addition, the Prosecutor has opened an investigation in Libya as well as preliminary examinations in Guinea, Nigeria, Côte d'Ivoire, and several countries outside of Africa, such as Afghanistan, Colombia, Georgia, Honduras, and the Republic of Korea. Although ICC prosecutions have been praised by human rights advocates, the perception that the Court has focused on Africa and the ICC Prosecutor's choice of cases have been controversial among leaders and commentators on the continent.

The Statute of the ICC, also known as the Rome Statute, entered into force on July 1, 2002, and established a permanent, independent Court to investigate and bring to justice individuals who commit war crimes, crimes against humanity, and genocide. As of October 2010, 114 countries— including 31 African countries, the largest regional block—were parties to the Statute. The United States is not a party.

Chapter 3- The International Criminal Court (ICC) is the first permanent international court with jurisdiction to prosecute individuals for "the most serious crimes of concern to the international community." Currently, 110 countries are States Parties to the ICC. Since its inception in 2002, the ICC has received three referrals for investigations by States Parties and one referral from the United Nations Security Council.

Chapter 4- The United States is not a party to the ICC, and is unlikely to become a party anytime soon. Nonetheless, the United States had interests at stake in the discussions at Kampala. The principal focus of the Kampala Conference was consideration of proposals to add to the ICC's jurisdiction a new crime of aggression, some of which could have seriously affected uses of military force by the United States and its allies. The United States also had an interest in better understanding the state of the ICC's work generally, and its prospects for making an effective contribution to promoting accountability for genocide, war crimes, and crimes against humanity. In this regard, the United States, under both the George W. Bush and Obama administrations, has supported the ICC's investigation of such crimes in Darfur, pursuant to a 2005 referral by the U.N. Security Council.

Chapter 5- As my colleague Ambassador Stephen Rapp noted earlier this week, the United States comes to this Conference in the spirit of renewed engagement, with the aims of supporting a constructive outcome that is based on consensus, that strengthens the Court as an institution, and that advances the cause of human rights and international criminal justice. We are engaged in a complex exercise of making international criminal law for the real world. To be a success, this Review Conference must promote a principled, workable system of international criminal justice that is consistent with existing international law and institutions and fair both to victims of abuse and to individuals who may eventually be prosecuted for the crime of aggression. We cannot credibly claim success if we produce an unworkable and divisive compromise that weakens the Court, diverts it from its core human rights mission, or undermines our multilateral system of peace and security.

Chapter 6- The conference completed three main tasks. It endorsed and supported the court's core work with respect to the traditional crimes of genocide, war crimes, and crimes against humanity, and highlighted issues of state cooperation, peace and justice, stocktaking, and participation of victims, about which Ambassador Rapp will say more. It also adopted two new crimes, prohibition and non-international armed conflict of certain weapons, the so-called Belgian amendment, and a crime of aggression whose elements will be reconsidered and affirmatively considered after seven more years.

In: International Criminal Court
Editor: Michael N. Baker

ISBN: 978-1-61324-694-8

Chapter 1

INTERNATIONAL CRIMINAL COURT AND THE ROME STATUTE: 2010 REVIEW CONFERENCE*

Matthew C. Weed

SUMMARY

ICC Review Conference and U.S. Engagement

The International Criminal Court (ICC, or Court) was established in 2002 as the first permanent court to prosecute war crimes, crimes against humanity, and genocide (together, "ICC crimes"). Pursuant to a provision in the Statute of the International Criminal Court ("Rome Statute" or "Statute"), the States Parties to the Rome Statute agreed to review the Court's activities seven years after its establishment. In compliance with this provision, the States Parties convened a Review Conference in Kampala, Uganda, May 31–June 11, 2010.

After declining to officially participate in the activities of the ICC or in the sessions of the Rome Statute's Assembly of States Parties (ASP) since the Court was established in 2002, the United States shifted its stance and began attending ASP meetings as an observer in November

* This is an edited, reformatted and augmented version of a Congressional Research Service 7-5700, www.crs.gov, R41682 publication, Prepared for Members and Committees of Congress, dated March 10, 2011.

2009, signaling a new policy of engagement with the ICC. At the Review Conference, the United States participated fully as an observer.

Issues Considered at the 2010 ICC Review Conference

Proposals in the Review Conference's agenda had broad possible ramifications for U.S. interests, and provided an opportunity for the United States to assess its policy toward the Court. Review Conference participants considered adding the crime of aggression to the ICC's jurisdiction, which would allow prosecution of state officials for using armed force against another state. The United States opposed this proposal for a number of reasons, including the possibility that U.S. officials might be prosecuted for their decisions. These concerns parallel the U.S. concerns over the possible prosecution of U.S. officials and servicemembers for the other ICC crimes. The question of ICC aggression jurisdiction was the most contentious for the Review Conference. States Parties argued over two central issues for activation of ICC aggression jurisdiction:

- whether both aggressor and victim state consent would be necessary to grant ICC jurisdiction over an instance of alleged criminal aggression; and
- the extent to which the U.N. Security Council should control the Court's exercise of aggression jurisdiction.

The States Parties adopted new jurisdiction provisions after several compromises, including delayed implementation and restricted application of the Court's aggression jurisdiction, and allowing states to opt out of ICC aggression jurisdiction.

The Review Conference agenda also included a number of discussions assessing the effect of the ICC on international criminal justice, especially with regard to crime victims and affected communities, and States Parties' cooperation with the ICC. During the Conference, the U.S. delegation demonstrated its new policy of engagement, pledging in-kind support for existing ICC cases and investigations, and for the development of States Parties' judicial-system capacity to prosecute ICC crimes. U.S. officials have since expressed support for the ICC, stating that it is now the global focal point for international criminal justice.

Possible Congressional Actions Concerning the New U.S.-ICC Policy

U.S. officials have asserted that this new policy of engagement with the ICC complies with U.S. law concerning the U.S.-ICC relationship, including the American Servicemembers' Protection Act of 2002 (ASPA), which was broadly intended to limit U.S. cooperation with and prohibit U.S. funding for the Court. In light of existing law and new ICC engagement, Congress may opt to take certain actions, including

- conducting hearings to better inform Members of Congress about
- the possibility of the United States becoming party to the Rome Statute in the wake of the changes to the Statute made at Kampala;
- the implications for U.S. interests, especially U.S.-servicemember security, of the adoption of ICC aggression jurisdiction;
- the new U.S.-ICC relationship; and
- executive branch compliance with the ASPA and other legislation;
- adding executive-branch reporting requirements on U.S. cooperation with the ICC and its basis in U.S. law, as well as developments in ICC practice related to changes in the Rome Statute adopted by the Review Conference; and
- amending existing legislation to direct the U.S.-ICC relationship, including dealing with ICC aggression jurisdiction and other changes to the Rome Statute.

Background

U.S. Policy Toward the ICC[1]

The International Criminal Court ("ICC" or "Court") is a permanent international court that currently has jurisdiction to prosecute individuals for war crimes, crimes against humanity, and genocide (together, "ICC crimes"). Cases may be referred to the Court by States Parties or by the U.N. Security Council, and the ICC prosecutor may on his own initiative request authorization to investigate possible ICC crimes. The ICC was created upon entry into force of the Statute of the International Criminal Court ("Rome Statute" or "Statute"), on July 1, 2002. One hundred and fourteen countries are States Parties to the Statute.[2] The United States, however, is not a party to the Statute.

The United States was an initial supporter of the creation of the ICC and played a major role at the international conference that negotiated and finalized the Rome Statute in 1998. President William J. Clinton signed the Rome Statute in 2000 but stated that he would not transmit it to the Senate requesting its advice and consent due to a number of U.S. concerns, primarily the potential for the ICC to assert jurisdiction over U.S. officials and members of the U.S. Armed Forces, even if the United States was not a Party to the Rome Statute. In May 2002, President George W. Bush notified the United Nations that the United States did not intend to become Party to the Rome Statute. The United States also concluded bilateral immunity agreements (BIAs) with approximately 100 countries. These BIAs were intended to fall within the provisions of Article 98 of the Statute, which exempts a state from surrendering individuals to the ICC if such actions would violate the international treaty obligations of that state.[3]

Congress passed legislation restricting U.S. cooperation with the ICC. On August 2, 2002, President George W. Bush signed the American Servicemembers' Protection Act of 2002 (ASPA).[4] It generally prohibits U.S. government cooperation with the ICC by

- restricting the use of appropriated funds to assist the ICC;
- restricting U.S. participation in certain U.N. peacekeeping operations due to possible ICC prosecution; and
- authorizing the President to free members of the U.S. Armed Forces and other individuals detained or imprisoned by or on behalf of the ICC.

Section 2015 of the act creates an exception from the prohibition on assisting the ICC in order to bring to justice foreign nationals accused of ICC crimes.[5]

The U.S. stance toward the Court seemed to soften during President George W. Bush's second term, as the United States began to treat the ICC as a potentially effective tool for international criminal justice. In 2008, for instance, the United States did not prevent adoption by veto of a U.N. Security Council resolution referring a war crimes case to the ICC prosecutor for investigation into atrocities in the Darfur region of Sudan.[6] Under the Obama Administration, U.S. officials have been generally supportive of the ICC, while cautioning that the United States maintains its concerns about the threat the Court poses to U.S. officials and members of the Armed Forces, and that U.S. ratification of the Statute is not currently an option. In November 2009, the United States for the first time attended a meeting of the Assembly of States Parties (ASP) of the International Criminal Court as an observer. Upon announcement of U.S. participation, Stephen Rapp, U.S. ambassador-at-large for war crimes issues, stated that "[the U.S.] government has now made the decision that Americans will return to engagement with the ICC."[7] At the November ASP meeting, Ambassador Rapp stated that the United States would also participate in the ICC Review Conference scheduled to take place in 2010.[8]

ICC Review Conference Planning and Agenda

Paragraph 1 of Article 123 of the Rome Statute requires the convening of a review conference:

> Seven years after the entry into force of this Statute the Secretary-General of the United Nations shall convene a Review Conference to consider any amendments to this Statute. Such review may include, but is not limited to, the list of crimes contained in article 5 [the crime of genocide; crimes against humanity; war crimes; and the crime of aggression]. The Conference shall be open to those participating in the Assembly of States Parties and on the same conditions.

Soon after the creation of the ICC, the ASP created a Working Group of the Review Conference to evaluate various issues, amendments, and potential agenda items for the required review conference. Several years of the Working Group's meetings and work provided guidance for the ASP's decision making concerning the Review Conference's agenda and the content of the proposed resolutions and other Review Conference agenda items. On November 21, 2008, the ASP adopted a resolution approving an application from the government of Uganda to hold the Conference in Uganda's capital, Kampala.[9] In two resolutions adopted November 26, 2009, and March 25, 2010, respectively, the ASP resolved to convene the Review Conference and determined the primary elements of the Review Conference's agenda.[10]

The agenda for the Review Conference included a number of issues and proposals slated for action by the States Parties, including making amendments to the Rome Statute. The central agenda item was consideration of new provisions to define and activate ICC jurisdiction over the crime of aggression, which involves actions of a state official or leader that cause the use of armed force against another state. The Review Conference would also consider a proposal to remove Article 124 from the Statute, which allowed a new State Party to exempt itself from ICC jurisdiction for the first seven years after becoming party to the Statute. In addition, there was a proposal to include within the definition of war crimes the use of certain poisonous or asphyxiating substances as well as certain types of bullets in non-international conflicts.[11] Finally, the agenda called for the Conference to convene discussions to take stock of the work of the ICC to date and its effects on international justice and other issues. These so-called "stocktaking" exercises included sessions on

- the obligations of States Parties to cooperate with the ICC and each other to effect international criminal justice;
- the efforts to improve States Parties' national judicial systems' respective capacity to prosecute individuals for war crimes, crimes against humanity, and genocide under the principle of "complementarity";[12]
- the effect of the Rome Statute system on victims of and communities affected by crimes under the ICC's jurisdiction; and
- the relationship between engaging in peace processes and pursuing international criminal justice.

Crime of Aggression

The central issue considered by the Review Conference was the proposed adoption of the crime of aggression into the jurisdiction of the Court. This section reviews the primary issues and points of contention concerning the ICC's proposed aggression jurisdiction. It includes

- an overview of different states' and other stakeholders' positions on the Court's aggression jurisdiction;
- a discussion of the proposed and adopted definition of the crime of aggression and the issues surrounding such definition; and
- a discussion of the provisions that set out the Court's jurisdiction over aggression, including the provisions as proposed, the main issues of contention for the Review Conference, and the jurisdictional provisions as they were ultimately adopted by the Conference.

During negotiations to finalize the Rome Statute in 1998, some countries' delegations to the conference wished to include aggression as one of the crimes under the ICC's jurisdiction in order to empower the ICC to end impunity for waging aggressive war in violation of international law generally and the U.N. Charter in particular. The participants could not agree on the definition and jurisdiction provisions of aggression, however, and thus included aggression as a crime included in the Rome Statute but not yet defined or activated. Article 5, paragraph 1 of the Rome Statute, lists the international crimes within the Court's jurisdiction: the crime of genocide, crimes against humanity, war crimes, and the crime of aggression. Paragraph 2 of Article 5 states that the Court will exercise jurisdiction over aggression after it has adopted a provision defining the crime and setting conditions for the exercise of jurisdiction over the crime. Article 123 states that such an addition to the Rome Statute must be considered and adopted at a Review Conference.

In anticipation of the Review Conference mandated by the Rome Statute, the ASP created a Special Working Group on the Crime of Aggression (SWG) in 2002. The SWG was tasked with creating working proposals for amendments to the Rome Statute defining the crime of aggression and the Court's exercise of jurisdiction over the crime. The context within which the SWG undertook its work presented a number of challenges. First, the Court's three operative crimes (war crimes, crimes against humanity, and genocide) had been prosecuted in numerous cases before ad hoc international criminal tribunals and national courts in the decades prior to their inclusion in the Rome Statute. Aggression jurisprudence, on the other hand, has been frozen since the late 1940s, when several German and Japanese officials were prosecuted under the crime of aggressive war. Since the advent of the Cold War, no aggression prosecutions have been undertaken. The SWG, therefore, had no clear and current international practice on which to rely with respect to defining and exercising jurisdiction over the crime of aggression when compared with the three more established crimes. Second, since the end of the Cold War, international recognition has expanded for certain uses of force, including foreign military action to stop atrocities taking place within the borders of a country. Overall, U.N.-mandated peacekeeping operations have greatly increased in number since 1991. Any consideration of prosecuting illegal uses of force is complicated by the growing acceptance of military action considered acceptable by the international community. Third, while war crimes, crimes against humanity, and genocide are *jus in bello* crimes, that is, crimes committed during an armed conflict, aggression is a *jus ad bellum* crime, involving a determination of the legality of the decision to initiate the armed conflict itself. Fitting a *jus ad bellum* crime into the established procedures and jurisdictional practice of three *jus in bello* crimes might prove difficult.

A number of observers and governments, including the United States, have voiced opinions over the perceived benefits and risks of including the crime of aggression in the ICC's jurisdiction, and the possible effect on the operation of the ICC overall. Leading up to and during the Review Conference, several States Parties, as well as the United States as observer, opposed adoption of jurisdictional provisions for aggression if consensus among States Parties could not be achieved.[13] Any decision taken without consensus, they argued, might result in permanent discord among States Parties and reduced State Party cooperation with the Court. There was sentiment among some participants that the Review Conference would be the last opportunity to activate aggression as an ICC crime; these participants believed that consensus was less important than adopting the provisions activating the aggression crime to reduce illegal military action as soon as possible. Analysts have also argued that the addition of a new crime at this point in the ICC's development might cause the Court to be overburdened with a set of new cases when it still has not completed a trial. In addition, some argued that adopting aggression might prevent the ICC from meeting the goal of universal acceptance of its jurisdiction, as several major powers, including the United States, China, Russia, and India, already had concerns about ICC jurisdiction over the crime. Activating aggression may cause one or more of these countries to foreclose the possibility of becoming States Parties to the Rome Statute. In addition, many, including State Department Legal Adviser Harold Koh, have argued that any determination over the propriety of military action is inherently political, and that the ICC would weaken its reputation as an impartial judicial body if it embroiled itself in political disputes between parties to armed conflict.[14]

In addition, U.S. officials have expressed concerns about the ICC's jurisdiction over aggression that are specific to the interests of the United States. These officials have pointed to the special position that the United States occupies as the "sole global superpower," and the fact that the United States is expected to use its military more frequently than other countries because in many instances it is uniquely capable of meeting international security challenges. If the ICC gains the ability to prosecute government officials for their decisions to take military action, they have argued, U.S. decision makers would be disproportionately at risk of prosecution, possibly for political reasons. U.S. officials and some analysts have asserted that with the ICC's activation of the crime of aggression, U.S. officials charged with making national and international security decisions might hesitate to initiate military action for fear of later ICC prosecution and punishment. Also, as with the three crimes currently operative under the Rome Statute, the Department of Defense has remained concerned over the possibility that the ICC will prosecute members of the U.S. Armed Forces for carrying out military operations abroad. Ambassador Rapp has stated that if these concerns are not properly addressed prior to adoption of new aggression provisions, the chances for universal acceptance of ICC jurisdiction by all countries, a primary goal of the ICC and its supporters, will be diminished.[15] Commentators have interpreted this to mean that the United States would not become party to the Rome Statute if aggression provisions are adopted that are not acceptable to the United States.[16]

During the Review Conference, the States Parties to the Rome Statute reached consensus on proposed amendments both to define the crime of aggression and to set out the circumstances and procedures under which the ICC may exercise jurisdiction over the crime. The following two sections evaluate the amendments as adopted in relation to arguments made and concerns expressed about such amendments, and the extent to which such concerns, especially those of the United States, were addressed by the Review Conference.

Definition of the Crime of Aggression

Over several years, the SWG developed the definition of the crime of aggression eventually proposed at the Review Conference, with the input of not only States Parties but also other stakeholders such as observer nations and relevant non-governmental organizations (NGOs). The definition of the act of aggression, which makes up part of the overall definition of the crime of aggression within the amendment, as well as a list of examples of uses of armed force constituting an act of aggression, are based on a U.N. General Assembly resolution adopted by consensus in 1974 with the general support of the United States.[17] It was widely accepted among observers that the SWG had succeeded in producing consensus among States Parties for the definition as proposed prior to the Review Conference, and the amendment was adopted at the Conference without changes.

Definition as Adopted[18]

As mentioned above, the definition adopted by the States Parties during the Review Conference defines both the "crime of aggression" and an "act of aggression." "Crime of aggression" is defined as

> the planning, preparation, initiation or execution, by a person in a position effectively to exercise control over or to direct the political or military action of a State, of an act of aggression which, by its character, gravity and scale, constitutes a manifest violation of the Charter of the United Nations.

"Act of aggression" as contained in the definition of "crime of aggression" is defined as

> the use of armed force by a State against the sovereignty, territorial integrity or political independence of another State, or in any other manner inconsistent with the Charter of the United Nations.

The definition then lists a number of acts that qualify as an act of aggression, in accordance with a list included in the 1974 U.N. General Assembly resolution. This list includes (1) military invasion or attack on another state's territory or any occupation or annexation of another state's territory; (2) bombardment or use of weapons against another state's territory; (3) blockading ports; (4) attacking another state's armed forces, including marine and air fleets; (5) use of armed forces in another state by agreement when such use violates the agreement; (6) aiding another state through use of territory to commit aggression against a third state; and (7) sending irregular forces into another state to use armed force.

Arguments and Concerns

Although States Parties and other stakeholders were generally satisfied with the definition of aggression developed by the SWG, a number of criticisms of the definition remained and were discussed prior to and during the Review Conference. Critics argued that the definition is vague and overly broad. Such perceived vagueness may be characterized as unfair to individuals whose actions might fall under the definition, because they cannot determine what actions are prohibited. Some observers have argued that the limited jurisprudence and precedent for aggression crimes increases the importance of clearly defining the crime of aggression within the Rome Statute, and that a vague definition could increase the chance that politically motivated prosecutions might take place.

Critics have offered an additional number of perceived problems with the definition:

- The definition does not adequately explain which individuals qualify as officials who may "exercise control over or direct the political or military action of a State," or what level of control such official must possess. There has been concern that lower-level commanders and officers may be swept into this definition, and that their decision making may be adversely affected if they believe they may be prosecuted by the Court.
- The definition makes it difficult to determine what type of military action rises to the level of a "manifest violation" of the U.N. Charter, and whether such a manifest violation can be found only when all three elements of "character, gravity, and scale" are first verified. Although there is a list of acts that would qualify as aggression, it is argued that the use of terms such as "however temporary" to describe prohibited actions may include small incursions in the definition of prosecutable aggression.
- The definition is overbroad, possibly sweeping in uses of force to stop war crimes and other atrocities in a state, enforcement of the responsibility to protect in countries where atrocities are taking place, and self-defense under Article 51 of the U.N. Charter.

Ambassador Rapp has stated that a definition limiting certain uses of force to stop atrocities could weaken the core human rights mission of the ICC, by essentially preventing military and political forms of human rights protection.[19] Other observers have disagreed with these criticisms, however, stating that the definition contains sufficient detail to properly describe actions that are prohibited, and that it will effectively limit prosecutions to only the highest ranking officials.

The U.S. delegation to the Review Conference concurred with many of the aforementioned concerns about and criticisms of the proposed definition. Given the definition's overall consensus support from States Parties and other stakeholders, and the United States' latecomer status in the process, the U.S. delegation accepted the definition's language. But it also promoted an interpretation of the language that would add further detail to the definition and protect U.S. interests.[20] As an annex to the resolution that adopted the amendment adding the definition of aggression, the States Parties included a list of "understandings" that are meant to guide the Court in interpreting the provisions added. Two of these understandings are intended to maintain a certain threshold for acts that may give rise to an aggression prosecution:

- The sixth understanding provides that aggression applies only to the "most serious and dangerous form of the illegal use of force" and that an aggression determination depends on "all the circumstances of each particular case." This language seems to be directed at minimizing the possibility that uses of force considered necessary to stop atrocities committed against civilian populations could constitute acts that might be prosecuted as aggression.
- The seventh understanding explains that determining whether an act of aggression constitutes a manifest violation of the U.N. Charter requires that there be acts of a sufficient character, gravity, and scale together to create such a violation. "No one component can be significant enough to satisfy the manifest standard by itself." This understanding addresses the concern that small incidents or incidents of short duration, most likely carried out through decisions of lower ranking officers, might otherwise be prosecuted for aggression under the adopted definition.

After the Conference, Legal Adviser Koh characterized these understandings as a suitable bulwark against prosecutions for low-level incidents, military activities undertaken to stop atrocities, and actions taken in self-defense.[21]

The States Parties also adopted elements of the crime of aggression in a separate annex to the aggression resolution; these elements further sharpened the adopted aggression definition in the Statute and the application of such definition to individuals. The annex states, among other things, that there is no requirement that an accused individual legally determine whether an act constitutes a manifest violation of or that it is inconsistent with the U.N. Charter. The elements include the requirement that an accused individual was aware of the factual circumstances that established that a use of force is inconsistent with and manifestly violates the U.N. Charter.[22]

Activation of Jurisdiction

Adoption of the new article activating the Court's jurisdiction over the crime of aggression was the most contentious and debated action taken at the Review Conference; negotiations were protracted and did not conclude until the Conference ended. The jurisdiction provision as proposed contained a number of alternative versions, with the final version to be worked out during the Conference. After contentious debate and numerous substantial revisions to the original proposals, the States Parties adopted new provisions to activate the ICC's jurisdiction over the crime of aggression.

The Conference participants debated two primary issues concerning the ICC's jurisdiction over aggression: whether a state must consent to the ICC's aggression jurisdiction over its nationals or territory, and whether and to what extent the U.N. Security Council should determine which aggression cases are heard by the Court.

Provision Activating Aggression Jurisdiction as Proposed

The provision proposed before the Review Conference began dealt primarily with the issue of where authority to initiate an aggression case before the Court would lie:

- with the Security Council only;
- with the Security Council and the ICC prosecutor; or
- with the Security Council and the prosecutor, subject to certain requirements and restrictions.

The proposed amendments contained two alternative versions of the jurisdiction activation provisions, each with a number of different options. In the first alternative, the provision stated that if the Security Council finds an act of aggression has occurred, the prosecutor may proceed with an investigation as to whether the act constitutes a crime of aggression; if the Security Council does not determine an act of aggression, the prosecutor may not initiate proceedings. Another option added that the prosecutor may initiate proceedings without a Security Council determination if the Security Council requests the prosecutor to conduct the investigation.

In the second alternative, the provision stated that prosecutor will notify the Security Council of a case of alleged aggression. The prosecutor is then authorized to initiate an investigation on his own if the Security Council does not make a determination whether or not an act of aggression has occurred in a certain case within six months of notification. Other options allowed the prosecutor to proceed with a case if he receives authorization from the ICC Pre-Trial Chamber, the U.N. General Assembly, or the International Court of Justice.

Issue: State Consent to ICC Aggression Jurisdiction

Adding aggression to the list of crimes under the jurisdiction of the ICC necessitated a determination of the situations that would require a state's consent to such jurisdiction, based either on the nationality of the individuals accused of aggression, or the territory of the state on which the aggression crime took place. Prior to and during the Conference, States Parties and other stakeholders advanced opposing arguments on the issue. Many asserted that the Court's jurisdiction over the crime of aggression should only require the consent of the state that is the victim of an act of aggression, arguing that jurisdiction for the other three ICC crimes is determined in this fashion. They claimed that to require aggressor state consent for aggression cases would weaken the system of international justice that the ICC is tasked to apply, which recognizes universal jurisdiction for certain serious crimes.

Others, including the United States, countered that the crime of aggression pertains directly to a state's official decisions to take military or other aggressive action, made in a political context. These decisions, they argued, are therefore unlike war crimes, crimes against humanity, and genocide, which pertain to actions taken during conflict and do not require high-level official state action for prosecution and conviction. They contended that each state, whether party to the Rome Statute or not, should be afforded the right to refuse consent to ICC aggression prosecutions of its nationals in order to preserve established rights of sovereignty over such official decisions. In addition, Legal Adviser Koh has argued that because aggressor state consent is considered necessary by some international law experts for aggression cases that might be conducted in the national court systems of another country, such consent should also be required for ICC aggression cases.[23]

The advent of ICC jurisdiction over aggression crimes has caused certain observers to warn against a possible proliferation of aggression cases in national courts through the ICC's principle of complementarity. Because crimes under the ICC's jurisdiction are universal jurisdiction crimes, any state may bring cases involving such crimes in their own national courts. Some have argued that if complementarity is applied to aggression cases, national courts of one state may seek to pass judgment on the official actions of another state, characterizing them as criminal aggression. Some states might bring such cases to trial for political reasons, these critics assert. If states believe their officials will be targeted for prosecution by other states' national court systems for politically motivated reasons, they might choose not to accept the ICC's or any other jurisdiction over the crime of aggression.

Issue: U.N. Security Council Role in ICC Aggression Cases

Some countries, led by the five permanent members of the U.N. Security Council (China, France, Russian Federation, United Kingdom, and United States), supported an activation provision that reserved jurisdiction determinations to the Security Council alone.[24] The majority of States Parties, most of which at any given time are not members of the Security Council, opposed a so-called "Security Council trigger" for ICC aggression cases. These countries include many of the non-aligned movement (NAM) group of countries, and developing countries generally, including many African nations.

Many arguments for sole Security Council authority over ICC aggression jurisdiction relate to the current role of the Security Council in curtailing and responding to acts of aggression under established international practice. Because the Security Council is vested with determining threats to international peace and security under Article 39 of the U.N. Charter, including determining whether an act of aggression has occurred, some have argued that the Security Council should also exercise sole discretion to allow ICC aggression cases to proceed. Some countries have argued that any aggression jurisdiction provision that allows initiation of investigations of aggression crimes without Security Council sanction would by definition violate international law. Legal Adviser Koh, presenting the current U.S. view, has warned that if the ICC prosecutor or other ICC body independently determines an act of aggression has occurred as a part of the judicial process leading to an aggression prosecution, such a determination may conflict with the Security Council's aggression determination concerning the same set of facts, leading to confusion in the international community on the criteria applied to determine aggression under international law.[25]

Many other countries and other stakeholders, however, state that the Security Council would in most cases be unwilling to take up deliberations to determine acts of aggression and to authorize ICC aggression investigations. They assert that even if allegations of possible cases of aggression were added to the Council's agenda, achieving the unanimity of the five permanent members to authorize aggression cases would be difficult, likely resulting in many deserving aggression cases never being investigated or prosecuted. In addition, some observers have disputed the assertion that the Security Council has the exclusive authority to determine an act of aggression, and that the U.N. Charter does not support such an exclusive role on aggression.

Opponents of sole Security Council authority to initiate ICC aggression cases or determine acts of aggression that might be prosecuted by the ICC also argue that such authority would damage the ICC's judicial independence; the ICC would be relying on an external political entity to determine its jurisdiction. In turn, they assert, this lack of independence could weaken the ICC as an institution, diminishing the effectiveness of the Court in prosecuting war crimes, crimes against humanity, and genocide, as well as aggression. Some have argued as well that any Security Council determination of an act of aggression prior to ICC prosecution would infringe on the Court's responsibility to determine an element of the crime of aggression, thereby prejudicing the ICC's work.

A number of arguments concerning the Security Council's role in determining ICC jurisdiction over aggression cases focus as well on the possible politicization of the crime of aggression under the Rome Statute. Some proponents of a "Security Council trigger" for ICC aggression jurisdiction argue that a finding of aggression is at heart a political determination, casting judgment on the political and military decision making of a state's officials and requiring a response from the Security Council, a political body. Because of its political nature, they maintain, the Security Council is best placed to determine whether aggression has occurred and whether any prosecutions for the crime of aggression should take place. Many opponents of such Security Council authority counter that it is precisely because the Security Council makes political determinations that it should not be involved in the judicial determinations of the ICC, and that any jurisdictional requirement involving the Security Council would necessarily taint judicial proceedings with political decisions. Therefore, while the Security Council is tasked with determining the international political and military response to acts of aggression, these observers have advocated the complete separation of the ICC's judicial process from the functions and decisions of the Security Council.

Provisions Activating Aggression Jurisdiction as Adopted

After contentious debate and several alterations to the originally proposed text, the States Parties at the Review Conference adopted two new articles for the Rome Statute, setting out the activation of the ICC's jurisdiction over the crime of aggression.[26] As will be explained in this section, these new provisions address the major concerns about state consent to aggression jurisdiction and Security Council authority over the ICC's exercise of such jurisdiction, and also contain provisions for delayed activation of aggression jurisdiction. The adopted provisions appear to represent major compromises and a strong desire to come to agreement on the part of the States Parties. For the United States, according to Legal Adviser Koh, the provisions, while not ideal, will provide the protections for U.S. servicemembers and officials that were desired by the U.S. delegation.[27]

New Provisions for Initiation of Aggression Cases

As with the other three crimes within ICC jurisdiction, aggression cases under the new provisions may be initiated by the following methods:

- A State Party may refer the case to the Court. If a State Party refers an act of aggression to the ICC, it must involve officials of a State Party and must have taken place in the territory of a State Party. If an aggressor State Party has opted out of aggression jurisdiction (as explained below), however, no aggression case can be initiated.
- The ICC prosecutor may initiate aggression proceedings. If the ICC prosecutor determines that an aggression case should proceed, a number of conditions and restrictions apply:
- First, like State Party referrals, if the case involves a non-party state's nationals or territory, or involves nationals of a State Party that has opted out of aggression jurisdiction (as explained below), the case cannot proceed.
- Second, the ICC prosecutor must ascertain whether the Security Council has determined that an act of aggression has occurred:
- If the Security Council has made such a determination, the prosecutor may proceed with an aggression investigation. The adopted provision states that an outside entity such as the Security Council may not

prejudice the independent judgment of the ICC in determining whether an act of aggression has occurred.

- If the Security Council makes no determination on whether an act of aggression has occurred, within six months of a notification by the prosecutor, the prosecutor may proceed with an investigation if the ICC's Pre-Trial Division authorizes commencement of such investigation.
- The Security Council may refer an aggression case. In the case of a Security Council referral, the Security Council may refer officials of any state for acts of aggression in any state, whether either pertinent state is party to the Rome Statute or not, and whether an involved State Party has accepted ICC aggression jurisdiction or not.

For all aggression cases, the Security Council retains the authority to defer commencement of aggression cases for one year under Article 16 of the Rome Statute, and can renew such deferment on an annual basis. The new provision thus reserves to the Security Council overriding, albeit limited, authority to prevent aggression cases going forward.

Delayed Implementation and Prospective Application to Aggression Crimes

Although the States Parties adopted the jurisdiction activation provisions for aggression during the Review Conference, they delayed the exercise of this jurisdiction. According to the new provisions, the ICC may not exercise jurisdiction over the crime of aggression until two-thirds of States Parties agree to such authority in "a decision to be taken after 1 January 2017." Thus, similar to the Rome Statute including aggression originally but delaying consideration of its definition and the ICC's jurisdiction over the crime, the aggression jurisdiction amendments as adopted at the Review Conference set out the Court's jurisdiction but delay its exercise. In addition, the Court may exercise jurisdiction only over those aggression crimes committed at least one year after the date that 30 States Parties have ratified or accepted the amendments activating jurisdiction over aggression. Pursuant to the understandings accompanying the aggression jurisdiction amendments and adopted by the States Parties, these two timing provisions read together allow the ICC to exercise jurisdiction only with respect to aggression crimes committed after the adoption of the amendments (on or after January 1, 2017) and after 30 States Parties accept the amendments, whichever is later.

Jurisdiction over Non-Party States and State Party Opt-out Provisions

The States Parties adopted jurisdiction activation provisions that allow states to be exempt from ICC aggression jurisdiction for situations referred to the Court by States Parties or requests from the ICC Prosecutor to investigate situations.[28] In these instances, the ICC cannot exercise jurisdiction in aggression cases involving the nationals or territory of states that are not States Parties of the Rome Statute. Also, if a State Party has previously declared that it does not accept the ICC's aggression jurisdiction, the Court may not initiate proceedings concerning an alleged aggression violation by that State Party's nationals or on that Party's territory. A State Party may make such a declaration prior to the expected 2017 activation of the ICC's aggression jurisdiction by two-thirds of the States Parties.

Understandings Concerning Complementarity as Applied to Aggression

The Rome Statute obligates States Parties to prosecute individuals in their respective national justice systems for the three crimes originally activated under the Statute: war crimes, crimes against humanity, and genocide. This obligation, and the status of the ICC as a court of last resort for prosecuting atrocity crimes, is termed complementarity. Under complementarity principles, the ICC will only prosecute individuals for these three crimes when no state with relevant jurisdiction over a crime can or is willing to prosecute. At the Review Conference, the States Parties adopted an understanding stating that the adoption of aggression jurisdiction does not create a right or obligation to prosecute individuals for aggression crimes under complementarity principles. This understanding addresses concerns about allowing countries to prosecute other countries' officials for state-sanctioned military and political decision making. Although understandings are not binding on States Parties, the fact that the States Parties adopted this understanding indicates general acceptance that aggression prosecutions and jurisprudence will be confined to the ICC; individual States Parties will not undertake such prosecutions. Some observers may assert that this understanding weakens the principle of universal jurisdiction of states to prosecute crimes associated with armed conflict under the Rome Statute, and unnecessarily creates different classes of crimes under the Statute.

U.S. Reaction to Aggression Jurisdiction Provisions as Adopted

U.S. officials who participated at the Review Conference have expressed general satisfaction with the aggression jurisdiction provisions adopted by the States Parties. Although the States Parties adopted provisions to make aggression operational under the Rome Statute, which the United States had originally wished to avoid, the United States as a non-party state cannot be subjected to ICC jurisdiction over cases initiated by State Party referral or the ICC prosecutor for aggression crimes that are allegedly committed on U.S. soil or by its nationals. The United States has veto power over any attempt to refer an aggression case through the U.N. Security Council. Thus, members of the U.S. Armed Forces or U.S. officials are not in danger of ICC aggression prosecution. Also, through action as a permanent member of the Security Council, the United States retains its ability to defer commencement of aggression cases on an annual basis under Article 16 of the Rome Statute.

In addition, because the ICC's exercise of jurisdiction over aggression has been delayed until 2017, U.S. officials have explained that the aggression provisions adopted may be opened to further debate. Ambassador Rapp and Legal Adviser Koh characterized the activation delay to 2017 as a "notional solution that can be reexamined" and a "non-final approach" to aggression, and has indicated that the United States will continue to engage through meetings of the ASP to improve the provisions on the definition of aggression and the ICC's aggression jurisdiction. Similarly, Ambassador Rapp called it a "deferral" of the aggression issue, and stated that the activation delay will allow the ICC to refocus on its core human rights mission, that is, on the original three ICC crimes.[29]

Optional Seven-Year Exemption from Jurisdiction

Article 124 of the Rome Statute, which is titled "Transitional Provision," provides that a State Party, during its first seven years as a Party, can declare that it does not accept the jurisdiction of the Court, effectively exempting from prosecution war crimes, crimes against humanity, and genocide committed by its nationals or on its territory for that time period. The provision also requires that the first Review Conference examine this Article's provisions. When the Rome Statute was originally finalized, contentious debate surrounded Article

124, because many saw it as potentially gutting the ability of the Court to effectively prosecute international crimes during its first several years. It was included to encourage certain states that were undecided about the Court to become Parties to the Rome Statute.

In the Review Conference agenda, the ASP included a proposal to delete Article 124 entirely. Supporters of this proposal argued the provision was meant to be "transitional" in nature, providing assurances to States Parties as the ICC began operations in 2002, and that it was no longer needed. The fact that Article 124's own language requires a review under Article 123, paragraph 1, which specifically relates to changes in the Rome Statute, seemed to support this view. Also, only two States Parties, France and Venezuela, availed themselves of the exemption, while numerous other States Parties have engaged in armed conflicts without finding an exemption declaration necessary. France withdrew its declaration prior to the end of the seven-year period, and Venezuela's seven-year exemption has expired. Proponents of deleting Article 124 argued further that removing an exemption option would reflect the ICC's growth as an entity and its importance under international law. Although there seemed to be wide support for this proposal, some argued that maintaining the exemption provided in Article 124 would encourage more states to become party to the Rome Statute, acting as an assurance to countries even if they do not find it necessary to activate their exemption rights. Although it might harm the cause of international criminal justice in the short term, they argued, it would increase the likelihood of eventual universal acceptance of the Court's jurisdiction.

The States Parties chose not to amend the Rome Statute to delete Article 124, so the right of new parties to exempt themselves for seven years remains. Japan and the European Union (EU) both touted its significance for eventual universal acceptance of ICC jurisdiction, and Japan in become States Parties in coming years.

Employing Certain Weapons In Non-International Conflicts

The ASP included a resolution for consideration at the Review Conference to add employing certain types of weapons in non-international conflicts to the definition of war crimes under Article 8(2)(e) of the Rome Statute. The new provisions would outlaw the following actions:

(xiii) Employing poison or poisoned weapons;

(xiv) Employing asphyxiating, poisonous or other gases, and all analogous liquids, materials or devices; and

(xv) Employing bullets which expand or flatten easily in the human body, such as bullets with a hard envelope which does not entirely cover the core or is pierced with incisions.

Identical provisions are already included in Article 8(2)(b) of the Statute, which applies to international conflicts. At the Review Conference most States Parties and other stakeholders supported adoption of these additional prohibitions in Article 8. The United States, however, had expressed concerns about these provisions, both for their possible application to actions taken by domestic authorities within the United States and for U.S. Armed Forces activities in conflicts such as Afghanistan and Iraq that were non-international in character. Rosa Brooks, Senior Advisor to the Under Secretary of Defense for Policy, stated in May 2010 that the amendments might not take into account the necessity of using certain types of weapons both in counter-terrorism operations, as well as some domestic law enforcement and public security activities. She also suggested that the rules on employment of certain weapons can be better regulated under existing international treaties on the use of conventional weapons.[30] Proponents of the new prohibitions argued that these prohibitions have already been established in international law through the custom and practice of the international community, and that their addition would reflect customary international law.

The States Parties adopted the new prohibitions for addition to Article 8(2)(e) at the Review Conference. In response, the U.S. as well as the Canadian and Israeli delegations supported a French delegation statement that interpreted the new prohibition concerning use of certain bullet types to prohibit their use only if there is a specific intent to aggravate suffering or wounding effect.[31] Interpreting the provisions to require a finding of such intent would raise the threshold for finding a violation of the provisions.

Stocktaking of International Criminal Justice

During the Review Conference, the States Parties and other stakeholders convened a number of panel and roundtable discussions to take stock of the state of international criminal justice as undertaken by the ICC, and to discuss and determine strategies concerning the effects of the ICC's work and State Party involvement in that work. Four main stocktaking topics were covered:

- cooperation of States Parties with the ICC and other States Parties in bringing criminals to justice;
- the principle of complementarity under the Rome Statute and its role in fighting impunity for atrocity crimes;
- the effect of the Court on victims of international crimes and affected communities; and
- the relationship between achieving peace and effecting justice for criminal actions committed during armed conflict.

As a result of these discussions, States Parties adopted resolutions concerning victims of crimes and complementarity, as well as a declaration concerning cooperation. The States Parties did not adopt a resolution or declaration on the topic of peace and justice.

Generally, observers of the stocktaking exercise at the Review Conference have asserted that it was a productive undertaking, even though it did not concern the central judicial and investigative operations of the Court. Instead, it focused on States Parties' obligations under the Rome Statute and highlighted the need to consider the effects of the ICC on issues outside mere prosecutions. These issues are often intertwined with the political will and governmental capabilities of States Parties and other states both to accept the jurisdiction of the ICC and to cooperate with the Court on individual cases. Although State Party and observer delegations made official statements during the stocktaking sessions, some have commented that the meetings were made more useful by allowing subject-matter experts, rather than state representatives, to lead many of the discussions. This, they claim, led to a sharpened focus on concrete strategies and practical approaches to improvement of the ICC's effectiveness.

The U.S. delegation participated fully as an observer in the stocktaking exercise. In the period before the Review Conference took place, many observers promoted U.S. involvement in the stocktaking meetings due to the capacity of the United States to assist the ICC both through diplomatic support and a number of technical areas of international criminal justice where the United States has long experience. During the Conference, it has been reported that the U.S. delegation played a central role in the stocktaking sessions, and the United States reportedly was the only non-party state to make specific pledges of support to improve work in the four areas discussed. Ambassador Rapp has stated that despite the restrictions in ASPA on the use of U.S. funds to support the ICC, the United States has provided in-kind technical assistance to the ICC and will continue to do so on a case-by-case basis.[32] Legal Adviser Koh has stated that such assistance does not require a change in U.S. law going forward.[33]

Cooperation

Part IX of the Rome Statute contains a number of provisions creating obligations for States Parties to cooperate with the Court as it investigates and prosecutes the crimes under its jurisdiction. Part X contains provisions concerning the role of States Parties in enforcing sentences handed down by the ICC. States Parties are required under the Statute to

- cooperate with the Court in general and in response to specific ICC requests for information and assistance,
- arrest wanted individuals, and
- ensure that they maintain and enforce national laws and procedures that will permit full cooperation with the ICC.

During the Review Conference, the States Parties, observer states, and other stakeholders met to discuss the experiences of the ICC and States Parties with respect to cooperation.

At the stocktaking exercise on cooperation, a number of salient issues arose. One of the central concerns involved the execution of arrest warrants. In addition, participants cited problems with cooperation stemming from the lack of States Parties' national legislation allowing cooperation and the incompatibility of national criminal procedures and the ICC's procedures. Ad hoc voluntary agreements between individual States Parties and the ICC were suggested as workarounds for national law deficiencies, especially in such matters as transfers of arrested individuals; enforcement of sentences; and relocation of witnesses, victims, and acquitted individuals. Some discussed the need to ensure that defense teams for those accused of crimes before the ICC receive equal assistance as prosecution teams.

Participants also highlighted the importance of ICC and State Party assistance to other States Parties to build capacity and pass legislation enabling them to fully cooperate with the Court. Some argued that certain States Parties faced significant obstacles both in terms of their respective national justice systems' ability to cooperate with the ICC, and the possible internal political fallout from such cooperation. In addition, some stressed the inability of the ICC to punish non-cooperative States Parties or to encourage other States Parties to shame or bully other states into cooperating, and expressed the hope that the ASP would act to persuade States Parties to improve their cooperation in the future.

After these meetings, the States Parties adopted a declaration emphasizing the obligations States Parties have to cooperate with the Court, especially in

- executing arrest warrants and complying with requests from the ICC;
- encouraging States Parties to enter into voluntary cooperation agreements with the Court; and
- sharing lessons learned from prior ICC cooperation experience with other States Parties, among other things.[34]

The States Parties also adopted a resolution to strengthen the enforcement of sentences handed down by the Court, calling on States Parties to indicate their willingness to receive sentenced individuals and recognizing that states generally may accept sentenced persons through cooperation with an international organization or mechanism.[35]

Ambassador Rapp has stated that the United States can foster ICC cooperation generally through its experience working with the ad hoc international criminal tribunals in the former Yugoslavia, Rwanda, and Sierra Leone, including in the operational areas of enforcing warrants, information sharing, and protecting witnesses, and can give diplomatic support for ICC cooperation in its dealings with other countries. ICC officials have stressed the importance of U.S. cooperation with the Court, especially with regard to providing resources necessary to locate, arrest, and transport accused individuals for ICC prosecution. U.S. officials have expressed the United States' intent to assist current ICC investigations into atrocities allegedly committed in Kenya during its 2009 elections. Ambassador Rapp and Legal Adviser Koh have stated their desire to ascertain the status of States Parties' cooperation with the ICC on investigations in the Democratic Republic of the Congo, the Central African Republic, Sudan, and Uganda. Ambassador Rapp has explained that past U.S. cooperation with ad hoc international tribunals is now shifting to cooperation with the ICC, as the Court is expected to replace the ad hoc international tribunals going forward, and he has stated that the

United States has "an abiding interest in seeing the Court successfully complete the prosecutions it has already begun."

Complementarity

The ICC was established as a judicial venue of last resort for war crimes, crimes against humanity, and genocide. Under the Rome Statute, States Parties are expected to arrest and prosecute those accused of these crimes, if their respective national courts have jurisdiction over such crimes. The ICC acts as a "complementary" judicial venue in case no State Party or nonparty state can or is willing to exercise jurisdiction over any allegation of these types of crimes.

During the Review Conference, the States Parties and other stakeholders held a stocktaking meeting on the issue of complementarity, specifically focusing on the need for States Parties to improve their overall capacity to prosecute ICC atrocity crimes in their respective national judicial systems. This focus on improving the capacity of national judicial systems to undertake prosecutions for ICC crimes has been termed positive complementarity. Participants discussed the importance of assisting States Parties needing to improve their national systems to prosecute ICC crimes. They noted that while the ICC serves as a backstop for States Parties when they cannot prosecute ICC crimes, the ICC is not designed nor has the capacity or resources to prosecute any more than the highest-level perpetrators of such crimes. The ICC prosecutor's investigations have demonstrated the ICC's intent to prosecute only the highest-level individuals accused of ICC crimes. Without States Parties prosecuting the higher number of middle- and lower-level actors alleged to committed ICC crimes, they say, an "impunity gap" is created that frustrates the overall goals of international justice. A number of experts and State Party representatives suggested approaches to improving national systems, including ensuring national criminal laws provide for prosecution of ICC crimes, and in some cases creating special national courts to prosecute alleged perpetrators of ICC crimes.

Participants also stressed the necessity of assisting States Parties to improve the capacity of their respective national systems. International organizations, especially the United Nations, it was explained, already provide such assistance, and States Parties, organized through the ASP, should do more to assist other States Parties. Although the ICC itself can aid States Parties through information sharing, some argued that the Court itself has limited resources and must concentrate primarily on its judicial work. The States Parties adopted a resolution on complementarity at the Review Conference that reiterated the primary role of States Parties to prosecute ICC crimes, expressed the need for additional measures to ensure that States Parties can prosecute ICC crimes, and called for greater international and state-to-state assistance to increase States Parties' ability to prosecute these crimes.[36] In addition, the resolution requests that the ASP Secretariat facilitate information sharing among the Court, States Parties, international organizations, and civil society to increase the capacity of the national judicial systems of States Parties.

Ambassador Rapp expressed U.S. support for the concept of positive complementarity, stating that the United States will aid the development of the capacity of other states' judicial systems to prosecute ICC crimes. This position is in general agreement with the U.S. government's position that war crimes and other atrocity crimes should be prosecuted by sovereign nations rather than international bodies when possible. According to U.S. officials, many U.S. rule-of-law programs and other programs to build judicial capacity already support positive complementarity principles for atrocity crimes. During the Review Conference, the United States stressed its major international role in judicial capacity building, co-sponsoring a program with Norway and the Democratic Republic of the Congo on efforts to improve the judicial capacity in that African country. The United States also pledged to continue aid to states for improvement of their national judicial systems. Some observers have argued that U.S. and other international assistance needs to include aid specifically to increase capacity to prosecute ICC crimes and share information with the ICC, and to aid passage of new national legislation for states that currently cannot effectively prosecute ICC crimes. Other have called for new funding for the ASP Secretariat to lead capacity building programs for States Parties needing assistance to achieve positive complementarity goals.

Impact on Victims and the Relationship between Peace and Justice

Meetings were held during the Review Conference on the impact of the ICC on victims and affected communities and on the issue of the relationship of international justice to efforts to bring peace to societies affected by war. During the meetings on victims, attendees lauded the rights in the Rome

Statute of victims to participate in ICC proceedings as more than just witnesses, and the ICC's role in "breaking the silence" of victims of atrocity crimes. Articles 68 and 75 of the Statute provide for participation of and reparations for victims of ICC crimes. Some argued, however, that efforts are needed to improve outreach to victims and affected communities, and to increase ICC field presence, to both inform them of their rights and the better inform and involve victims in the ICC process. Some participants also proposed increasing assistance to victims for physical and psychological rehabilitation through the ICC's Trust Fund for Victims, created under Article 79 of the Rome Statute, which receives donations from States Parties on a voluntary basis. Concerning the Trust Fund generally, some participants argued that States Parties need to increase contributions, especially to fund measures to support women victims who often must continue to live in the same areas as the perpetrators of such crimes against women even after the crimes have occurred.

At the Conference's stocktaking meeting concerning peace and justice issues, some participants argued that the existence and activities of the ICC have contributed to the rejection of the concept that achieving peace and ensuring justice in armed conflicts are necessarily at odds with each other. It has long been suggested that attempting to arrest and prosecute leaders involved in armed conflict and alleged to have committed atrocity crimes will convince such leaders to refuse any political settlement and to continue conflicts indefinitely, because they expect to be incarcerated in prosecutions that may be politically motivated. Some claimed that the Court, while slow in its process, has sent a signal that impunity for atrocity crimes will no longer be tolerated and should no longer be used as a bargaining chip in peace negotiations. It was also claimed that the Court's pursuit of justice had in fact aided some peace processes by marginalizing individuals accused of crimes who were obstacles to political settlement. Failing to ensure justice for criminal acts, some argued, diminished the durability of peace settlements in certain situations, because animosity toward such perpetrators undermined societies' capacity to sustain political compromise between former warring groups. It was recognized that justice measures undertaken by the ICC may still need to be sequenced carefully to avoid undermining peace efforts, and that U.N. Security Council deferments of prosecutions under Article 16 of the Rome Statute may be necessary. Participants also recognized that the ICC must be aided by national and local transitional justice measures and non-judicial initiatives in order to effectively strengthen lasting peace. Other attendees, however, reiterated concerns that ICC activities could delay peace settlements going forward.

The States Parties adopted a resolution at the Review Conference on the impact of the Rome Statute system on victims and affected communities, highlighting first the need for States Parties to preserve the rights and protections for victims provided in the Rome Statute through national legislation.[37] The resolution also calls on the Court to increase its accessibility to victims through better outreach and an augmented field presence. It encourages greater State Party funding for the Trust Fund for Victims and cooperation among States Parties, the ICC, and the Trust Fund Secretariat to coordinate promotion of the importance of Trust Fund activities. In addition, the resolution calls on national governments, communities, and civil society to act to sensitize societies to victims' rights, especially victims of sexual violence, and the importance of anti-stigmatization and reintegration programs for such victims. With regard to peace and justice, the States Parties did not adopt a resolution or declaration, but expressed the need to continue discussing and monitoring the issue in future ASP sessions.

Issues and Options for Congress

The outcomes of the Review Conference present a number of issues related to the authorities and operation of the ICC, and to the relationship between the ICC and the United States. The States Parties adopted changes to the Rome Statute that increased the Court's jurisdiction, most importantly by adding the crime of aggression to the ICC's list of prosecutable crimes. This occurred despite some objection, including that of United States. It seems clear, however, that the States Parties to the Rome Statute as a whole are heavily in favor of moving forward with expanding the ICC's role in international criminal justice, expanding the influence of international criminal justice generally. The decisions taken at Kampala seem to signify the States Parties' continued expectation that the ICC will grow as an important tool in encouraging peaceful resolution of disputes and discouraging military and other leaders from engaging in unlawful military activities, both at the beginning of and during armed conflicts.

With regard to U.S. interests, the U.S. delegation to the Review Conference did not condemn the addition of aggression and other provisions to the Rome Statute. The provisions defining the Court's jurisdiction over the crime seem to exclude U.S. officials and members of the U.S. Armed Forces from prosecution for the crime of aggression, and U.S. delegation efforts to clarify the definition of aggression under the Rome Statute make it likely that only the most serious cases of aggressive military action might be subject to prosecution. With regard to U.S. officials and servicemembers possibly being subjected to ICC prosecution for war crimes, crimes against humanity, and genocide, however, the Review Conference did not alleviate these long-standing U.S. concerns, and the Obama Administration has repeatedly asserted that the United States will not seek to become a party to the ICC in the near future.[38]

The Review Conference nevertheless showed that the United States is actively engaging with the ICC, and intends to participate fully with the ASP on major issues regarding the Rome Statute and the operations of the Court. The Obama Administration's official policy toward the ICC is one of engagement as an observer nation, with further participation to come during the periodic meetings of the ASP. U.S. officials at the Review Conference made pledges of in-kind support to the ICC regarding the Court's current cases and the ICC prosecutor's current investigations. Ambassador Rapp and Legal Adviser Koh expressed their desire to meet with the ICC prosecutor to determine what U.S. support can be provided. They have explained that their cooperative efforts comport with pertinent U.S. law and that they do not require, nor will the Administration request, amendments to such law, including ASPA.

Despite these assertions, Congress may decide to further examine the ICC and the U.S.-ICC relationship, both in terms of current and historic U.S. policy and as it relates to the restrictions and intent of ASPA. Congress might undertake some or all of the following.

- *Conduct hearings.* Congress might choose to gather further information on
    - U.S. engagement and cooperation efforts with the ICC, including the specific activities undertaken by respective executive agencies to cooperate with the ICC and the identified "in-kind" assistance to the ICC, including assistance that flows through international organizations such as the United Nations. Congress may also ask for an explanation of Administration policy and ICC cooperation as it relates to the intended restrictions on the U.S.-ICC relationship in ASPA;
    - the possibility of the United States becoming party to the Rome Statute in the wake of the adoption of the crime of aggression and

the restrictions on intrastate use of certain asphyxiating gases and special ammunition; and
- o the implications for U.S. interests, especially the security of members of the U.S. Armed Forces, of the adoption of provisions to activate the Court's jurisdiction over the crime of aggression.

- *Require executive branch reports.* Congress might consider requiring the executive branch to report on a periodic basis on
  - o U.S. cooperation with the ICC, including resources and personnel involved in such cooperation. As explained above, ASPA prohibits the use of appropriated funds to support the ICC, but the Obama Administration has pledged only "in-kind" assistance to the Court. Reporting on U.S. support for the ICC could shed light on whether U.S.-ICC cooperation activities fall within existing legislative authorities and restrictions, especially those in ASPA; and
  - o developments in the practices, procedure, and precedents of the ICC, as well as the statements of the ICC Prosecutor and other ICC officials, in relation to preparing for prosecuting the crime of aggression, as well as any ICC investigations into the actions of U.S. officials or officials of U.S. allies.
- *Amending existing or enact new legislation.* Because official U.S. policy toward the Court has shifted to one of engagement and support, Congress might provide direction to U.S. officials concerning the U.S.-ICC relationship going forward through new legislation, including provisions specifically dealing with the Review Conference's adoption of the crime of aggression and other changes to the Rome Statute. Such legislation might provide new authorities for or limitations on U.S. involvement with the Court, and might address the definition of "in-kind assistance" and U.S. provision of it to the ICC. Congress might decide to take up legislation that would provide policy direction on U.S. support or opposition to ICC activities and to delineate authorization for U.S. participation in meetings of the ASP and other U.S.-ICC engagement.[39]

End Notes

[1] For more information on the ICC and historic U.S. policy toward the Court, see CRS Report R41116, The International Criminal Court (ICC): Jurisdiction, Extradition, and U.S. Policy,

by Emily C. Barbour and Matthew C. Weed; CRS Report RL31437, International Criminal Court: Overview and Selected Legal Issues, by Jennifer K. Elsea; and CRS Report RL31495, U.S. Policy Regarding the International Criminal Court (ICC), by Jennifer K. Elsea.

[2] The Statute has 114 States Parties as of January 20, 2011. U.N. Treaty Collection, Multilateral Treaties Deposited With the Secretary-General, Ch. XVIII (Penal Matters), entry 10, http://treaties.un.org/pages/ViewDetails.aspx?src=TREATY&mtdsg_no=XVIII-10&chapter=18&lang=en.

[3] For a list of BIAs, see Georgetown Law Library, International Criminal Court — Article 98 Agreements Research Guide, http://www.ll.georgetown.edu/guides/article_98.cfm.

[4] Title II of P.L. 107-206; 22 U.S.C. §§ 7421–7433.

[5] 22 U.S.C. § 7433.

[6] U.N. Security Council Resolution 1593 (2005), March 31, 2005.

[7] As reported. BBC News, "US to resume engagement with ICC," November 16, 2009, http://news.bbc.co.uk/2/hi/8363282.stm.

[8] As reported. Colum Lynch, "US to Attend, but Not Join, ICC Conference," Washington Post, November 17, 2009, p. A20.

[9] Resolution ICC-ASP/7/Res.2, available at http://www.icc-cpi.int/Menus/ASP/Resolutions / Sessions/ 2008+-+7th+Session.htm.

[10] Resolution ICC-ASP/8/Res.6 and Resolution ICC-ASP/8/Res.9, available at http://www.icc-cpi.int/Menus/ASP/Resolutions/Sessions/2009+-+8th+Session.htm.

[11] These weapons were already included in the definition of war crimes as applied to international conflicts.

[12] For a description of the principle of complementarity, see "Understandings Concerning Complementarity as Applied to Aggression" below.

[13] Vijay Padmanabhan, From Rome to Kampala: The U.S. Approach to the 2010 International Criminal Court Review Conference, Council on Foreign Relations Special Report, Apr. 2010, p. 15; Harold Hongju Koh, legal adviser, U.S. Department of State, statement at the Review Conference of the International Criminal Court, June 4, 2010, http:// www. state. gov/s/l/releases/remarks/142665.htm.

[14] Harold Hongju Koh, legal adviser, U.S. Department of State, statement at the Resumed Eighth Session of the Assembly of States Parties of the International Criminal Court, Mar. 23, 2010, http://usun.state.gov/briefing/statements/2010/139000.htm.

[15] Stephen Rapp, U.S. ambassador-at-large for war crimes issues, statement at the opening of the 2010 Review Conference of the Rome Statute of the International Criminal Court, June 1, 2010, p. 9, http://www.icc-cpi.int/iccdocs/asp_docs/RC2010/Statements/ICC-RC-gendeba-USA-ENG.pdf.

[16] Brett Schaefer, "Trouble for the International Criminal Court," National Review Online, June 8, 2010, http://www.nationalreview.com/articles/229906/trouble-international-criminal-court / brett-d-schaefer.

[17] A/RES/3314 (XXIX), adopted Dec. 14, 1974.

[18] For full text, see RC/Res. 6, Annex I, para. 2, http://www.icc-cpi.int/iccdocs/asp_docs/Resolutions/RC-Res.6-ENG.pdf.

[19] American Society of International Law, presentation of Harold Hongju Koh, legal adviser, Department of State at U.S. Policy Toward the upcoming International Criminal Court Review Conference, May 14, 2010, p. 7.

[20] See Harold Hongju Koh, legal adviser, U.S. Department of State, statement at the Review Conference of the International Criminal Court, June 4, 2010, http://www.state.gov/s/l/ releases/remarks/142665.htm.

[21] Harold Hongju Koh, legal adviser, U.S. Department of State, statement at a press conference on the outcomes of the ICC Review Conference, June 15, 2010, http://www.state.gov /s/wci/us_releases/remarks/143178.htm.

[22] For full text, see RC/Res. 6, Annex II (elements of crimes amendments) and Annex III (understandings amendments), http://www.icc-cpi.int/iccdocs/asp_docs/Resolutions/RC-Res.6-ENG.pdf.

[23] Harold Hongju Koh, legal adviser, U.S. Department of State, statement at the Resumed Eighth Session of the Assembly of States Parties of the International Criminal Court, Mar. 23, 2010, http://usun.state.gov/briefing/statements/2010/139000.htm.

[24] The U.N. Security Council has five permanent members and 10 non-permanent members elected by the U.N. General Assembly to two-year terms. For further information, see http://www.un.org/Docs/sc/.

[25] Harold Hongju Koh, legal adviser, U.S. Department of State, statement at the Resumed Eighth Session of the Assembly of States Parties of the International Criminal Court, Mar. 23, 2010, http://usun.state.gov/briefing/statements/2010/139000.htm.

[26] For full text, see RC/Res. 6, Annex I, paras. 3 and 4, http://www.icc-cpi.int/iccdocs/asp_ docs/ Resolutions/RC-Res.6-ENG.pdf.

[27] Harold Hongju Koh, legal adviser, U.S. Department of State, statement at a press conference on the outcomes of the ICC Review Conference, June 15, 2010, http://www. state.gov/s/ wci/us_releases/remarks/143178.htm.

[28] As mentioned previously, U.N. Security Council referral grants ICC jurisdiction over nationals of any state regardless of their status as a Party to the Rome Statute or their acceptance of the Court's aggression jurisdiction.

[29] For both Legal Adviser Koh's and Ambassador Rapp's comments, see press conference on the outcomes of the ICC Review Conference, June 15, 2010, http://www.state.gov /s/ wci/ us_releases/remarks/143178.htm.

[30] American Society of International Law, statements of Rosa Brooks, Senior Advisor to the Under Secretary of Defense for Policy, at U.S. Policy Toward the upcoming International Criminal Court Review Conference, May 14, 2010, pp. 10, 23.

[31] See RC/11, Review Conference of the Rome Statute of the International Criminal Court: Official Records, Annex VI, statement B (France), p. 120.

[32] American Society of International Law, statement of Ambassador-at-Large for War Crimes Issues Stephen J. Rapp, at U.S. Policy Toward the upcoming International Criminal Court Review Conference, May 14, 2010, p. 13.

[33] Statement of Harold Hongju Koh, legal adviser, Department of State, at briefing on the International Criminal Court Conference in Kampala, Uganda, June 2, 2010, http://www.state.gov/s/wci/us_releases/remarks/142585.htm.

[34] Declaration RC/Decl.2, http://www.icc-cpi.int/iccdocs/asp_docs/Resolutions/RC-Decl.2-EN G. pdf.

[35] Resolution RC/Res.3, http://www.icc-cpi.int/iccdocs/asp_docs/Resolutions/RC-Res.3-ENG. pdf.

[36] Resolution RC/Res.1, http://www.icc-cpi.int/iccdocs/asp_docs/Resolutions/RC-Res.1-ENG. pdf.

[37] Resolution RC/Res.2, http://www.icc-cpi.int/iccdocs/asp_docs/Resolutions/RC-Res.2-ENG. pdf.

[38] See, e.g., statements of Stephen J. Rapp, ambassador-at-large for war crimes issues, and Harold Hongju Koh, legal adviser, Department of State, at press conference on the outcomes of the ICC Review Conference, June 15, 2010, http://www.state.gov/s/ wci/us_ releases /remarks /143178.htm.

[39] Legislation was proposed in the 111th Congress dealing in part with these issues. The American Self-Defense Protection Act of 2010 (H.R. 5351; 111th Cong.), introduced by Rep. Ileana Ros-Lehtinen on May 20, 2010, contains a provision prohibiting the use of appropriated funds for U.S. participation at "any [ICC] review conference or meeting of the Assembly of States Parties." It also provides a sense of Congress provision recommending that the President and Secretary of State lead diplomatic efforts to seek alternatives to the ICC and avoid any action that legitimizes the Court.

In: International Criminal Court
Editor: Michael N. Baker

ISBN: 978-1-61324-694-8

Chapter 2

INTERNATIONAL CRIMINAL COURT CASES IN AFRICA: STATUS AND POLICY ISSUES*

Alexis Arieff, Rhoda Margesson, Marjorie Ann Browne, and Matthew C. Weed

SUMMARY

The International Criminal Court (ICC) has, to date, opened cases exclusively in Sub-Saharan Africa. Twenty-two cases are currently before the ICC, all of them pertaining to crimes allegedly committed in five African states: Kenya, Sudan (Darfur), Uganda (the Lord's Resistance Army, LRA), the Democratic Republic of Congo, and the Central African Republic. The ICC Prosecutor has yet to secure any convictions. In addition, the Prosecutor has opened an investigation in Libya as well as preliminary examinations in Guinea, Nigeria, Côte d'Ivoire, and several countries outside of Africa, such as Afghanistan, Colombia, Georgia, Honduras, and the Republic of Korea. Although ICC prosecutions have been praised by human rights advocates, the perception that the Court has focused on Africa and the ICC Prosecutor's choice of cases have been controversial among leaders and commentators on the continent.

The Statute of the ICC, also known as the Rome Statute, entered into force on July 1, 2002, and established a permanent, independent Court to

* This is an edited, reformatted and augmented version of a Congressional Research Service 7-5700, www.crs.gov, RL34665 publication, Prepared for Members and Committees of Congress, dated March 7, 2011.

investigate and bring to justice individuals who commit war crimes, crimes against humanity, and genocide. As of October 2010, 114 countries— including 31 African countries, the largest regional block— were parties to the Statute. The United States is not a party.

One of the individuals sought by the ICC is Sudan's President Omar Hassan al-Bashir, who is accused of war crimes, crimes against humanity, and genocide in Darfur. The prosecution is the first attempt by the ICC to pursue a sitting head of state. The case has drawn praise from advocates but inspired a backlash among African states, who were previously supportive of the Court. Like Libya, Sudan is not a party to the ICC, and jurisdiction was granted through a United Nations Security Council resolution. Controversy within Africa has also erupted over ICC attempts to prosecute senior Kenyan officials in connection with that country's post-election violence of 2007-2008. Although Kenya is a state party to the Court and initially supported ICC engagement, some fear the prosecutions could be destabilizing. Obama Administration officials have expressed support for ICC prosecutions in both Sudan and Kenya, while stressing local authorities' primary responsibility in ensuring justice and accountability for abuses.

Congressional interest in the work of the ICC in Africa has arisen in connection with concern over gross human rights violations on the African continent and beyond, along with broader concerns over ICC jurisdiction and U.S. policy toward the Court. At the ICC's recent review conference in Kampala, Uganda, Obama Administration officials reiterated the United States' intention to provide diplomatic and informational support to ICC prosecutions on a case-by-case basis. Legislation introduced during the 111th Congress referenced the ICC in connection with several African conflicts and, more broadly, U.S. policy toward, and cooperation with, the Court.

This report provides background on current ICC cases and examines issues raised by the ICC's actions in Africa.

RECENT DEVELOPMENTS

- On February 26, U.N. Security Council Resolution 1970 referred the situation in Libya since February 15 to the International Criminal Court (ICC). This action provides the ICC with jurisdiction over war crimes, crimes against humanity, and genocide occurring in Libya since that date, even though Libya is not a state party to the Court.[1] On March 3, the ICC Prosecutor, Luis Moreno-Ocampo, announced he was initiating a formal investigation. The Prosecutor indicated he would focus on the role of the government and security forces in ongoing violence, but warned that members of armed opposition groups could also be held criminally liable for abuses.[2]

- An African Union (AU) backlash against the ICC has continued, although African countries make up a sizable block of states parties to the Court. At an AU summit in January 2011, the AU Assembly endorsed Kenya's request for a deferral of prosecutions there (which could only be enacted through action by ICC judges or at the U.N. Security Council). AU Commission chairman Jean Ping also accused the ICC Prosecutor of relying on "double standards" with regard to Africa. (See "Accusations of Bias," below.)
- The ICC trial of accused Congolese warlord Thomas Lubanga Dyilo (see "Thomas Lubanga Dyilo," below) was allowed to proceed on February 23, after ICC appeals judges overruled the third attempt by the defense to stay the proceedings.
- On January 25, Callixte Mbarushimana, a Rwandan national sought by the ICC for alleged war crimes and crimes against humanity in neighboring Congo, was transferred to ICC custody from France (see "Callixte Mbarushimana," below). The government of Rwanda, previously a vocal opponent of the Court, has welcomed the prosecution but stated that it would have preferred to try Mbarushimana within Rwanda on charges related to the 1994 genocide.

BACKGROUND

Overview of the International Criminal Court

The Statute of the ICC, also known as the Rome Statute (the Statute), entered into force on July 1, 2002, and established a permanent, independent Court to investigate and bring to justice individuals who commit war crimes, crimes against humanity, and genocide.[3] The ICC's jurisdiction extends over crimes committed since the entry into force of the Statute. The ICC is headquartered in The Hague, Netherlands. As of March 2010, 111 countries were parties to the Statute.[4] The United States is not a party to the ICC. The ICC's Assembly of States Parties provides administrative oversight and other support for the Court, including adoption of the budget and election of 18 judges, a Prosecutor (currently Luis Moreno-Ocampo from Argentina), and a Registrar (currently Bruno Cathala from France).[5]

As outlined in the Statute, situations[6] may be referred to the ICC in one of three ways: by a state party to the Statute, the ICC Prosecutor, or the United Nations (U.N.) Security Council. Currently, four situations have been publicly referred to the Prosecutor. The governments of three countries (all parties to the ICC)—Uganda, the Democratic Republic of Congo, and the Central African Republic—have referred situations to the Prosecutor. The U.N. Security Council has referred one situation (Darfur, Sudan) to the Prosecutor. One situation, Kenya, is under investigation following an application by the ICC Prosecutor. At least six others remain under consideration.[7]

The ICC is considered a court of last resort—it will only investigate or prosecute cases of the most serious crimes perpetrated by individuals (not organizations or governments), and then, only when national judicial systems are unwilling or unable to handle them. This principle of admissibility before the Court is known as "complementarity."[8] Although many domestic legal systems grant sitting heads of state immunity from criminal prosecution, the Statute grants the ICC jurisdiction over any individual, regardless of official capacity.[9]

The U.S. Position on the ICC

The United States is not a party to the Rome Statute. The United States signed the Statute on December 31, 2000, but at the time, the Clinton Administration had objections to it and said it would not submit it to the Senate for its advice and consent to ratification. The Statute was never submitted to the Senate. In May 2002, the Bush Administration notified the United Nations that it did not intend to become a party to the ICC, and that there were therefore no legal obligations arising from the signature. The Bush Administration opposed the Court and renounced any U.S. obligations under the treaty. Objections to the Court were based on a number of factors, including

- the Court's assertion of jurisdiction (in certain circumstances) over citizens, including military personnel, of countries that are not parties to the treaty;[10]
- the perceived lack of adequate checks and balances on the powers of the ICC prosecutors and judges;
- the perceived dilution of the role of the U.N. Security Council in maintaining peace and security; and

- the ICC's potentially chilling effect on America's willingness to project power in the defense of its interests.

The Bush Administration concluded bilateral immunity agreements (BIAs), known as "Article 98 agreements," with most states parties to exempt U.S. citizens from possible surrender to the ICC.[11] These agreements are named for Article 98(2) of the Statute, which bars the ICC from asking for surrender of persons from a state party that would require it to act contrary to its international obligations.

The U.S. government is prohibited by law from providing material assistance to the ICC in its investigations, arrests, detentions, extraditions, or prosecutions of war crimes, under the American Servicemembers' Protection Act of 2002, or ASPA (P.L. 107-206, Title II). The prohibition covers, among other things, the obligation of appropriated funds, assistance in investigations on U.S. territory, participation in U.N. peacekeeping operations unless certain protections from ICC actions are provided to specific categories of personnel, and the sharing of classified and law enforcement information.[12] Section 2015 of ASPA (22 U.S.C. 7433, known as the "Dodd Amendment"), however, provides an exception to these provisions:

> Nothing in this title shall prohibit the United States from rendering assistance to international efforts to bring to justice Saddam Hussein, Slobodan Milosevic, Osama bin Laden, other members of Al Qaeda, leaders of Islamic Jihad, and other foreign nationals accused of genocide, war crimes or crimes against humanity.

In her confirmation hearing as Secretary of State before the Senate Foreign Relations Committee in January 2009, Hillary Clinton said, "Whether we work toward joining or not, we will end hostility toward the ICC and look for opportunities to encourage effective ICC action in ways that promote U.S. interests by bringing war criminals to justice."[13] Speaking in Nairobi, Kenya, in August 2009, Secretary of State Clinton said that it was a "great regret" that the United States was not a party to the ICC, but that the United States has supported the Court and "continue[s] to do so."[14] Obama Administration officials have recently indicated, amid a wider review of U.S. policy toward the Court, that the Administration is "considering ways in which we may be able to assist the ICC, consistent with our law, in investigations involving atrocities."[15] A January 2010 review by the Department of Justice concluded that diplomatic or "informational" support for "particular investigations or prosecutions" by the ICC would not violate existing laws.[16]

In November 2009, the United States began formally attending meetings of the ICC's Assembly of States Parties as an observer nation, and in May 2010 sent a delegation led by Ambassador-at-Large for War Crimes Issues Stephen Rapp and State Department Legal Advisor Harold Koh to the Review Conference of the Rome Statute in Kampala, Uganda. Administration officials reiterated at the Conference the United States' intention to support current cases before the ICC. In addition, Rapp stated that Administration officials had "renewed our commitment to the rule of law and capacity-building projects in which we have ongoing in each" African country in which ICC prosecutions are taking place. At the same time, Rapp averred that the Administration was "nowhere near that point" of submitting the Rome Statute for ratification.[17]

The ICC and other International Courts and Tribunals

The post-World War II Nuremberg and Tokyo tribunals to prosecute Nazi and Japanese leaders for crimes against peace, war crimes, and crimes against humanity established precedent for other *ad hoc* international courts and tribunals, such as the International Criminal Tribunals for the former Yugoslavia[18] and for Rwanda.[19] In addition, the United Nations authorized the creation of a Special Court for Sierra Leone (SC-SL) to prosecute those with the greatest responsibility for serious violations of international humanitarian law and domestic law committed in the territory of Sierra Leone since November 30, 1996.[20] Separate judicial mechanisms have also been set up for cases involving East Timor (Timor-Leste) and Cambodia. Further, the U.N. Security Council authorized establishment of a Special International Tribunal for Lebanon in 2007, which began functioning in March 2009.

These courts and tribunals are distinct from the ICC. While established by the U.N. Security Council to address allegations of crimes against humanity in various countries, these tribunals were case-specific, limited in jurisdiction, and temporary. By contrast, the ICC was established by multilateral treaty and is a permanent, international criminal tribunal. It is not a U.N. body.[21]

International Court of Justice

The International Court of Justice (ICJ), also located in The Hague, is the principal judicial organ of the United Nations. The ICJ does not prosecute individuals; its role is to settle, in accordance with international law, legal disputes submitted to it by states. Only states may submit cases for consideration, although the ICJ will also give advisory opinions on legal questions when requested to do so by authorized international organizations.[22]

Congressional Interest in ICC Activities in Africa

Members of Congress have taken a range of positions on the ICC with regard to Africa. Many in Congress are concerned about massive human rights violations on the continent, and some see the ICC as a possible means of redress for these crimes. At the same time, many Members oppose the Court on jurisdictional and other grounds. For example, several pieces of draft legislation introduced during the 111th Congress, such as H.R. 5351 (Ros-Lehtinen), S.Con.Res. 59 (Vitter), and H.Con.Res. 265 (Lamborn), express broad objections to the ICC and to U.S. cooperation with it. S.Con.Res. 71 (Feingold) stated that it is in "the United States national interest" to help "prevent and mitigate acts of genocide and other mass atrocities against civilians," but did not explicitly reference the ICC.

Draft legislation introduced during the 111th Congress referenced the ICC in connection with human rights abuses committed in the Democratic Republic of Congo and by the Lord's Resistance Army in central Africa, and in connection with the global use of child soldiers. Additionally, there has been particular congressional interest in the ICC's work related to Darfur.

ICC Cases and Investigations in Africa

The ICC Prosecutor has opened cases against 23 individuals in connection with five African countries. Twenty-two of these are active; the twenty-third, against Darfur rebel leader Bahar Idriss Abu Garda, was dismissed by judges, though the prosecutor may attempt to submit new evidence to re-open it. The cases stem from investigations into Kenya's post-election violence in 2007-2008, rebellion and counter-insurgency in the Darfur region of Sudan, the Lord's Resistance Army insurgency, civil conflict in eastern Democratic Republic of Congo (DRC), and conflict in the Central African Republic. A sixth investigation has been opened in connection with Libya, after the U.N. Security Council referred the situation to the ICC on February 26, 2011.

Restrictions on U.S. Assistance to African Parties to the ICC

Jurisdictional and other concerns led Congress to pass ASPA (P.L. 107-206, Title II), which was signed into law on August 2, 2002. Section 2007 of ASPA prohibited U.S. military assistance to ICC member-states, except for NATO countries, major non-NATO allies, and countries subject to various other waiver provisions. Permanent waivers were granted to countries that ratified Article 98 agreements promising not to surrender U.S. nationals to the Court (see *Appendix*). However, despite continuing opposition among some Members, a combination of presidential waivers and changes to the law have effectively nullified restrictions on U.S. assistance to African parties to the ICC.

In Sub-Saharan Africa, ASPA effectively froze International Military Education and Training (IMET), Foreign Military Financing (FMF), and Excess Defense Articles (EDA) accounts for Kenya, Mali, Namibia, Niger, South Africa, and Tanzania. However, President Bush waived the prohibition on IMET assistance to 21 countries, including these six, on September 29, 2006, citing concerns that the restrictions could preclude valuable military-to-military ties.[23] Congress repealed the ASPA restriction on IMET funding in the National Defense Authorization Act for FY2007 (P.L. 109-364), which was signed into law on October 17, 2006. The National Defense Authorization Act for FY2008 (P.L. 110-181), signed into law on January 28, 2008, repealed Section 2007 of ASPA entirely, ending remaining prohibitions on FMF and EDA assistance.

Separately, the Nethercutt Amendment to the FY2005 Consolidated Appropriations Act (P.L. 108-447) prohibited Economic Support Fund (ESF) assistance to ICC parties that had not entered into an Article 98 agreement with the United States, with certain waiver provisions. This prohibition was included as part of the FY2006 Consolidated Appropriations Act (P.L. 109-102, Section 574), and was subsequently carried over via continuing resolutions on February 15, 2007 (P.L. 110-5) and September 29, 2007 (P.L. 110-92). A substantially identical restriction was included in the Consolidated Appropriations Act of 2008 (P.L. 110-161, Section 671), signed into law December 26, 2007. However, in practice, this restriction was not applied to African countries, due to presidential waivers with respect to Kenya, Mali, Namibia, Niger, South Africa, and Tanzania.[24] The Omnibus Appropriations Act of 2009 (P.L. 111-8) did not carry forward Section 671, ending such restrictions on ESF assistance.

The Prosecutor is also examining a military crackdown on opposition supporters in Guinea, ongoing violence in Côte d'Ivoire, and inter-communal violence in central Nigeria, but has not opened formal investigations or opened any cases in these countries.

Uganda, DRC, CAR, Kenya, Nigeria, and Guinea are states parties to the ICC. Sudan, Libya, and Côte d'Ivoire are not. ICC jurisdiction in Sudan and Libya stems from U.N. Security Council actions; jurisdiction in Côte d'Ivoire was granted by virtue of a declaration submitted by the Ivorian Government on October 1, 2003, which accepted the jurisdiction of the Court as of September 19, 2002.[25] Five suspects—four Congolese nationals and one Rwandan—are currently in ICC custody. The ICC Prosecutor has sought summonses, rather than arrest warrants, in connection with attempted prosecutions of Darfuri rebel commanders and of Kenyan suspects. The Prosecutor has not secured any convictions to date.

Kenya

On December 15, 2010, the Prosecutor presented two cases, against a total of six individuals, for alleged crimes against humanity. The Prosecutor has applied to ICC judges for summonses, rather than arrest warrants, stating that he believes summonses are sufficient to ensure the suspects' appearance before the Court.[26] The cases are related to post-election violence in Kenya in 2007- 2008, in which over 1,000 individuals were killed and a range of other abuses, including sexual violence, were allegedly committed. A government of national unity was formed following the disputed elections, and the issue of accountability for abuses has remained a sensitive one in Kenyan politics. The Prosecutor contends that high-ranking officials planned and instigated large-scale abuses, a view supported by independent investigations into the violence.[27]

The suspects named in the first case are William Ruto, Member of Parliament and former Minister of Education; Henry Kosgey, Minister of Industrialization; and Joshua Arap Sang, a radio journalist. Those named in the second case are Francis Muthaura, head of the public service, secretary to the Cabinet, and chairman of the National Security Advisory Committee; Uhuru Kenyatta, deputy prime minister and minister of finance; and Mohamed Hussein Ali, former commissioner of the Kenyan police. The suspects in the first case are associated with Prime Minister Raila Odinga, while those in the second case are associated with President Mwai Kibaki.

Odinga has expressed support for ICC involvement, while Kibaki has criticized it and called for trials to be held within Kenya instead.

Table 1. Summary of ICC Activities in Africa

Situation	Case	Status
Kenya	Politician William Ruto, Minister of Industrialization Henry Kosgey, and journalist Joshua Arab Sang	Summonses issued on December 15, 2010.
	Deputy Prime Minister Uhuru Kenyatta, Cabinet Secretary Francis Muthaura, and Maj. Gen. (Retd.)	Summonses issued on December 15, 2010.
Darfur, Sudan	Former Interior Minister Ahmad Muhammad Harun and alleged former militia leader Ali Kushayb	Arrest warrants issued in May 2007. Suspects at large.
	Darfur rebel leaders Bahar Idriss Abu Garda, Abdallah Banda Abakaer Nourain, and Saleh	Prosecutor's case against Abu Garda dismissed by ICC judges in February
	Sudanese President Omar Hassan al-Bashir	Arrest warrant issued in March 2009 for war crimes and crimes against
"Situation of the Lord's Resistance	LRA commanders Joseph Kony, Vincent Otti, Okot Odhiambo, Dominic	Arrest warrants unsealed in October 2005. Otti and Lukwiya reportedly dead.
Democratic Republic of Congo	Alleged militia leader Thomas Lubanga Dyilo	Suspect transferred to ICC custody in March 2006. Trial initiated in January 2009.
	Alleged militia leaders Germain Katanga and Mathieu Ngudjolo Chui	Suspects transferred to ICC custody in October 2007 and February 2008, respectively. Joint trial
	Former militia and rebel leader turned DRC army officer Bosco Ntaganda	Arrest warrant issued in August 2006, unsealed in April 2008. Suspect at large.

Situation	Case	Status
	Alleged militia leader Calixte Mbarushimana	Arrested in France in October 2010 and transferred to ICC custody on January 25, 2011.
Central African Republic	Former Congolese rebel leader turned Congolese transitional vice president and Senator Jean-Pierre Bemba Gombo	Suspect transferred to ICC custody in July 2008. Trial initiated in November 2010.
Situation	Case	Status
Libya	-	Jurisdiction granted by the U.N. Security Council in February 2011. Investigation opened on
Guinea	-	Preliminary examination.
Côte d'Ivoire	-	Preliminary examination.
Nigeria	-	Preliminary examination.

The prosecutions, which have targeted the upper echelons of political power, are an extremely sensitive issue in Kenya with potential implications for the country's stability, inter-ethnic relations, and elections scheduled for 2012. The ICC Prosecutor appeared to acknowledge this sensitivity by naming suspects of different ethnic groups and political loyalties. Several suspects, while maintaining their innocence, have stated that they will appear voluntarily before the court, and polls indicate that a majority of Kenyans support ICC prosecutions and believe that suspects should resign from government posts.[28] Still, the case has sparked a backlash within Kenya's political class. In December, parliamentarians have passed legislation urging Kenya to withdraw from the Court. (According to legal analysts, a withdrawal would not necessarily preclude ICC jurisdiction over crimes committed during the period when Kenya was a state party.) Kenyan officials have also lobbied the AU to call for a deferral by the U.N. Security Council.

The Kenyan government has pledged to cooperate with ICC actions, although senior officials were perceived by some observers as attempting to stonewall the investigation. Some Kenyans are reportedly concerned that prosecutions could stir up the same ethnic tensions that led to the post-election turmoil, while others fear that a lack of prosecutions could lead to future electoral violence.[29] Other concerns center around the protection and relocation of witnesses and victims, who have already reportedly been subjected to intimidation and threats.[30] In August 2010, Kenya came under criticism from advocates when it welcomed Sudanese President Bashir (see "The Case Against Bashir," below) to a celebration of the country's adoption of a new constitution.

Background on ICC Involvement

The Prosecutor's request to open an investigation in Kenya was approved by ICC judges in March 2010. Kenya is a party to the ICC, but it is the first instance in which ICC judges have authorized an investigation based on a recommendation from the Prosecutor, as opposed to a state referral or U.N. Security Council directive.

ICC involvement in Kenya follows protracted domestic wrangling over how to ensure justice for victims of the electoral violence without upsetting the government's fragile power-sharing agreement. An official investigation into the post-election violence, known as the Waki Commission, identified potential suspects and recommended the establishment of an independent Kenyan tribunal with international participation. In December 2008, the government accepted the Waki Commission's findings and agreed that it would refer the situation to the ICC if the Commission's recommendations were not implemented. Donors, including the United States and the European Union, expressed support for an independent domestic tribunal, and the Kenyan parliament was expected to pass legislation establishing such a tribunal by March 2009. In July 2009, however, legislation had yet to be passed, prompting chief mediator Koffi Annan, the former U.N. Secretary-General, to submit a list of individuals suspected of orchestrating the violence to the ICC. The Kenyan Cabinet subsequently announced that it would not establish a special tribunal, but would instead convene a "Truth, Justice and

Reconciliation Commission" (TJRC) which would not prosecute suspects but rather to oversee reforms in the judiciary, police, and other investigatory bodies that may, in turn, deal with the issue.[31]

U.S. Reactions

The United States initially expressed support for domestic prosecutions of suspects in postelection violence, but has supported ICC involvement in the absence of domestic action. Upon the Prosecutor's announcement of six suspects, President Obama stated, "I urge all of Kenya's leaders, and the people whom they serve, to cooperate fully with the ICC investigation and remain focused on implementation of the reform agenda and the future of your nation."[32] In February, U.S. Deputy Secretary of State James Steinberg said, "We are very committed to the principle of accountability and the avoidance of impunity and right now the only mechanism to pursue that is through the ICC." He added, "That is the choice the Kenyan government made when both the executive branch and the legislature chose not to pursue a domestic approach."[33]

Sudan

Sudan is a unique case because of the circumstances of ICC involvement and because of whom the ICC Prosecutor has chosen to pursue. ICC jurisdiction in Sudan was conferred by the U.N. Security Council, as Sudan is not a party to the Court. In September 2004, the Security Council had established an International Commission of Inquiry on Darfur under Resolution 1564, maintaining that the Sudanese government had not met its obligations under previous Resolutions.[34] In January 2005, the Commission reported that it had compiled a confidential list of potential war crimes suspects and "strongly recommend[ed]" that the Security Council refer the situation to the ICC.[35]

In 2005, the U.N. Security Council referred the situation in Darfur to the ICC Prosecutor. Following the referral, the ICC Prosecutor received the document archive of the Commission of Inquiry and the Commission's sealed list of individuals suspected of committing serious abuses in Darfur, though this list is not binding on the selection of suspects. The Office of the Prosecutor initiated its own investigation in June 2005. The Sudanese government also created its own special courts for Darfur in an apparent effort to stave off the ICC's jurisdiction; however, the courts' efforts have been widely criticized as insufficient.[36]

U.N. Security Council Resolution 1593

On March 31, 2005, the U.N. Security Council, acting under Chapter VII of the U.N. Charter, adopted Resolution 1593 (2005), which referred reports about the situation in Darfur, Sudan (dating back to July 1, 2002) to the ICC Prosecutor.[37] Under the ICC Statute, the ICC was authorized, but not required, to accept the case.[38] The Resolution was adopted by a vote of 11 in favor, none against, and with four abstentions—the United States, China, Algeria, and Brazil.[39] While Sudan is not a party to the ICC and has not consented to its jurisdiction, the Resolution is binding on all U.N. member states, including Sudan.

The U.S. Position on U.N. Security Council Resolution 1593

In statements made in July and September 2004, respectively, Congress and the Bush Administration declared that genocide was taking place in Darfur.[40] The Administration supported the formation of the International Commission of Inquiry for Darfur.[41] However, the Bush Administration preferred a special tribunal in Africa to be the mechanism of accountability for those who committed crimes in Darfur. It objected to the U.N. Security Council referral to the ICC because of its stated objections to the ICC's jurisdiction over nationals of states not party to the Rome Statute.[42] However, the United States had at one time supported a version of the Rome Statute that would have allowed the U.N. Security Council to refer cases involving non-states parties to the ICC, but would not have allowed other states or the Prosecutor to refer cases.

The United States abstained on Resolution 1593 (which is not equivalent to a veto in the Security Council) because the Resolution included language that dealt with the sovereignty questions of concern and essentially protected U.S. nationals and other persons of non-party States other than Sudan from prosecution.[43] The abstention did not change the fundamental objections of the Bush Administration to the ICC. At the same time, the Bush Administration supported international cooperation to stop atrocities occurring in Darfur.[44]

Ahmad Muhammad Harun and Ali Kushayb

In May 2007, the ICC publicly issued arrest warrants for former Interior Minister Ahmad Muhammad Harun and Ali Muhammad Ali Abd-Al-Rahman

(Ali Kushayb), an alleged former Janjaweed leader in Darfur.[45] They were each accused of over 40 counts of war crimes and crimes against humanity in connection with abuses allegedly committed in Darfur in 2003 and 2004. The Sudanese government refused to comply with either warrant. Although news reports suggest Sudanese authorities arrested Kushayb in October 2008, Sudanese officials stated they would conduct their own investigation into his alleged crimes in Darfur, and did not indicate that they planned to turn him over to the ICC.[46] In May 2009, Harun was appointed governor of South Kordofan State. In June 2010, the ICC Pre-Trial Chamber informed the U.N. Security Council that "the Republic of Sudan is failing to comply with its cooperation obligations stemming from Resolution 1593 (2005) in relation to the enforcement of the warrants of arrest issued by the Chamber against Ahmad Harun and Ali Kushayb."[47]

Darfuri Rebel Commanders

In December 2007, the ICC Prosecutor announced the opening of a new investigation into the targeting of peacekeepers and aid workers in Darfur. In November 2008, the Prosecutor submitted a sealed case against three alleged rebel commanders in Darfur whom he accused of committing war crimes during an attack on the town of Haskanita on September 29, 2007. Twelve African Union peacekeepers were allegedly killed and eight injured in the attack.[48]

In May 2009, ICC pretrial judges issued a summons to one of the three suspects, Bahar Idriss Abu Garda, to appear before the Court.[49] Abu Garda reported to The Hague voluntarily, where he denied the accusations of involvement in the Haskanita incident. In February 2010, ICC judges declined to confirm the Prosecutor's case, contending that there was insufficient evidence to establish that Abu Garda could be held criminally responsible for the attack on peacekeepers. In June 2010, the two remaining rebel commanders sought by the Prosecutor, Abdallah Banda Abakaer Nourain and Saleh Mohammed Jerbo Jamus, voluntarily surrendered to the Court. Their names had not previously been made public. Banda, a former military commander in the rebel Justice and Equality Movement (JEM), and Jerbo, a former leader in the Sudan Liberation Movement (SLM)-Unity faction, each face accusations of three counts of war crimes.

The Case against Bashir

On March 4, 2009, ICC judges issued an arrest warrant for Sudanese President Omar Hassan alBashir. The warrant holds that there are "reasonable grounds" to believe Bashir is criminally responsible for five counts of crimes against humanity and two counts of war crimes, referring to alleged attacks by Sudanese security forces and pro-government militia in the Darfur region of Sudan during the government's six-year counter-insurgency campaign. The ICC warrant states that there are reasonable grounds to believe attacks against civilians in Darfur were a "core component" of the Sudanese government's military strategy, that such attacks were widespread and systematic, and that Bashir acted "as an indirect perpetrator, or as an indirect coperpetrator."[50] In his application for an arrest warrant, filed in July 2008, the ICC Prosecutor affirmed that while Bashir did not "physically or directly" carry out abuses, "he committed these crimes through members of the state apparatus, the army, and the Militia/Janjaweed" as president and commander-in-chief of the Sudanese armed forces.

The arrest warrant is not an indictment; under ICC procedures, charges must be confirmed at a pre-trial hearing. The decision to issue a warrant is expected to take into account whether there are reasonable grounds to believe that a suspect committed crimes as alleged by the Prosecutor and whether a warrant is necessary to ensure the suspect's appearance in court. Although many domestic legal systems grant sitting heads of state immunity from criminal prosecution, the Rome Statute grants the ICC jurisdiction regardless of official capacity.[51]

Human rights organizations hailed the warrant, the first issued by the ICC against a sitting head of state, as an important step against impunity. Many governments, including France, Germany, Canada, the United Kingdom, and Denmark, and the European Union, have called on Sudan to cooperate. Reactions by African and Middle Eastern governments have been more critical, with many condemning the ICC or calling for the prosecution to be deferred. The governments of Russia and China have also expressed opposition.

The ICC urged "all States, whether party or not to the Rome Statute, as well as international and regional organizations," to "cooperate fully" with the warrant.[52] However, most observers agree that there is little chance of Bashir being arrested. One analysis noted that while Bashir may risk arrest if he travels overseas, "no one expects Sudan to hand over Bashir, who has been executive ruler of the country for more than 15 years, absent major political changes in the country."[53]

Sudanese government officials have rejected the ICC's jurisdiction, though some legal experts argue that Sudan is obligated as a U.N. member state to cooperate because the warrant stems from a U.N. Security Council resolution under Chapter VII.[54]

Genocide Accusations[55]

In his application for an arrest warrant in July 2008, the ICC Prosecutor accused Bashir of three counts of genocide, making the Sudanese president the first individual to be accused of this crime before the Court. The Prosecutor alleged that Bashir "intends to destroy in substantial part the Fur, Masalit and Zaghawa ethnic groups as such" through coordinated attacks by government troops and Janjaweed militia.[56] In 2009, ICC judges found, by a ruling of two-to-one, that the Prosecutor had "failed to provide reasonable grounds to believe that the Government of Sudan acted with specific intent" to destroy these groups.[57] The Prosecutor appealed, and on July 12, 2010, ICC judges issued a second warrant for Bashir, this time citing three counts of genocide. The second warrant does not replace, revoke, or otherwise alter the first warrant, which also remains in effect.[58]

Many human rights advocates welcomed the attempt to bring genocide charges. However, the formulation of the Prosecutor's accusation has drawn some criticism. The U.N. Commission of Inquiry concluded in its January 2005 report that the violence in Darfur did not amount to genocide, although "international offences such as the crimes against humanity and war crimes that have been committed in Darfur may be no less serious and heinous than genocide."[59] Some Darfur activists accused the Commission of allowing political considerations to affect its conclusions.[60] However, some critics contend that the Prosecutor's application concerning genocide did not sufficiently establish intent or Bashir's alleged role.[61]

Sudanese Reactions

The Bashir Administration has rejected ICC jurisdiction over Darfur as a violation of its sovereignty and accused the Court of being part of a neocolonialist plot against a sovereign African and Muslim state.[62] The Bashir administration has portrayed the ICC as an instrument of Western pressure for regime change, has repeatedly denied that genocide or ethnic cleansing is taking place in Darfur, and has accused the Prosecutor of basing his investigation on testimony by rebel leaders and "spies" posing as humanitarian workers.[63] The government has barred ICC personnel from speaking to Sudanese officials, and authorities have taken a hard-line stance against Sudanese suspected of sympathizing with the ICC prosecution attempt.[64] The government also responded by expelling over a dozen international aid organizations that it accused of collaborating with the ICC, including Oxfam and Doctors Without Borders.[65] In July 2010, when a second ICC warrant was issued for Bashir, Sudan expelled two senior humanitarian officials from Darfur. In November, Sudanese security forces attempted to shut down an independent radio station operating in Darfur whose staff they accused of working for the ICC and Darfuri rebels.[66]

Reactions to the warrant among Sudanese opposition groups have varied. Islamist opposition leader (and former Bashir ally) Hassan Al-Turabi criticized the government's stance toward the ICC and called on the president to turn himself over to the international justice system.[67] Other Sudanese opposition members have displayed measured support for Bashir while privately acknowledging mixed reactions.[68] Three major Darfur rebel factions—the Sudan Liberation Movement (SLM), Sudan Liberation Army (SLA), and Justice and Equality Movement (JEM)— welcomed the arrest warrant.[69] Reports suggest the Sudan People's Liberation Movement (SPLM)—the former southern rebel group and partner in the Government of National Unity under the 2005 Comprehensive Peace Agreement (CPA)—is ambivalent about the attempt to prosecute Bashir.[70] The SPLM initially called on the government "to cooperate with [the] ICC on the legal processes."[71] However, after the arrest warrant was issued, the SPLM released a statement saying that "Sudan should stand with Bashir at this hard time."[72] Some SPLM officials are reportedly concerned that ICC actions could endanger the CPA, while others have expressed hope that prosecution could leverage international pressure on Khartoum.[73]

A *New York Times* analysis noted that while many advocates hope the arrest warrant will weaken Bashir's hold in power, "Sudanese resentment of the court's actions could have the reverse effect and rally the nation to his side. After the court's prosecutor first announced that he was seeking a warrant for Mr. Bashir, some of the president's political enemies closed ranks behind him."[74]

Analysts disagree over whether the warrant has intensified Bashir's international isolation. The Sudanese leader has engaged in aggressive diplomatic outreach to allied states, traveling to multiple friendly countries in the weeks following the warrant's issuance.

Regional Reactions

The Sudanese government has rallied support from many Arab and African leaders, and among regional organizations such as the African Union (AU), the Arab League, the Community of Sahel-Saharan States (CEN-SAD), and the Organization of the Islamic Conference (OIC), all of which have criticized the ICC and called (unsuccessfully to date) for a deferral of prosecution by the U.N. Security Council. Some African and Middle Eastern commentators and civil society groups have praised the decision to pursue Bashir as a step against impunity in the region, while others expressed concern that the move displayed bias or a neocolonial attitude toward Africa.[75] In October 2009, an AU panel on Darfur led by former South African President Thabo Mbeki concluded that a special "hybrid" court, consisting of Sudanese and international judges, should try the gravest crimes committed in Darfur, but did not take a position on whether such a court would seek to try cases currently before the ICC. (This proposal has not been carried out to date.)

The decision to prosecute an African head of state has notably sparked a backlash among African governments, 31 of which are parties to the Court. In July 2009, the AU resolved not to cooperate with the ICC in carrying out Bashir's arrest. AU heads of state adopted a similar resolution in July 2010, after a second warrant for Bashir was issued, this time for the crime of genocide.[76] At the same time, African parties to the ICC have refrained from withdrawing from the Court.[77] On July 27, 2010, African heads of state participating in an African Union (AU) summit in Uganda approved a resolution condemning the ICC warrant for Sudanese President Omar Hassan alBashir, calling on AU member states to refrain from arresting the Sudanese president, and rejecting the ICC's request to open a liaison office at the AU headquarters in Addis Ababa, Ethiopia. The government of Botswana, a party to the ICC, has rejected the AU stance toward the Bashir case, and reports suggest wavering positions by the governments of Uganda and South Africa.[78]

Bashir has traveled to numerous countries in the region since the first ICC warrant was issued in 2009, including Egypt, Ethiopia, Libya, Qatar, Saudi Arabia, and Zimbabwe, none of which are parties to the ICC. In July 2010, Bashir traveled to neighboring Chad, his first trip to an ICC state party; although Chad had previously publicly supported the ICC prosecution, authorities declined to arrest him amid a broader attempt to improve historically strained bilateral relations between the two states. In August, Bashir traveled to Kenya—also an ICC state party, and one in which an ICC investigation is ongoing—and Kenyan authorities likewise declined to effect an arrest. Still, the warrants appear to have had some impact on Bashir's international movements, and reports in December 2010 suggested that he chose not to attend independence celebrations in the Central African Republic and an 80-country Africa-Europe summit meeting in Libya due to diplomatic pressures.

U.S. Reactions

The Obama Administration has expressed support for the ICC investigation and prosecution of war crimes in Sudan, and Administration officials have repeatedly stated that those responsible for serious crimes in Darfur should be held accountable. In July 2009, the Obama Administration's Special Envoy on Sudan, retired General J. Scott Gration, stated that U.S. engagement with Sudan in the context of peace negotiations "does not mean that [Bashir] does not need to do what's right in terms of facing the International Criminal Court and those charges."[79] In response to a question at an August 2009 press conference in Nairobi, Kenya, Secretary of State Hillary Clinton said, "The actions by the ICC sent a clear message that the behavior of Bashir and his government were outside the bounds of accepted standards and that there would no longer be impunity.... The United States and others have continued to support the need to eventually bring President Bashir to justice."[80] In July 2010, Gration nonetheless suggested that the ICC's decision to issue a second arrest warrant for Bashir "will make my mission more difficult and challenging."[81] President Obama subsequently stated in an interview that "it is a balance that has to be struck. We want to move forward in a constructive fashion in Sudan, but we also think that there has to be accountability, and so we are fully supportive of the ICC."[82] In August, Obama expressed "disappointment" that Kenya had hosted Bashir "in defiance of International Criminal Court arrest warrants."[83]

Administration officials have at times appeared to express divergent characterizations of the situation in Darfur. In June 2009, Special Envoy Gration suggested at a press briefing that the Sudanese government was no longer engaged in a "coordinated" genocidal campaign in Darfur, contending that ongoing violence represented "the remnants of genocide" and ongoing fighting between rebel groups, the Sudanese government, and Chadian actors.[84] Previously, U.N. Ambassador Susan Rice had characterized Darfur as a "genocide." In response to questions following Gration's remarks, a State Department spokesman stated, "I think there is no question that genocide has taken place in Darfur. We continue to characterize the circumstances in Darfur as genocide."[85] In July 2009, President Obama referred to Darfur as a "genocide," calling it a "millstone around Africa's neck."[86]

Congressional Reactions

Members of the 111th Congress expressed a range of positions with regard to the warrant for Bashir. Senator Russell Feingold urged the Administration not to defer the ICC prosecution, stating, "If there is significant progress made toward ending violence on the ground in Darfur, it may be appropriate to consider a suspension at that time."[87] Senator John Kerry stated the warrant "complicates matters," but should not stop U.S. efforts to resolve the conflict in Darfur.[88] In remarks on behalf of the Congressional Black Caucus, Congresswoman Barbara Lee commented, "it's so important to do the right thing now, which is to support the International Criminal Court in its efforts to hold Sudan's President Bashir accountable for his crimes against humanity." Several pieces of draft legislation introduced during the 111th Congress expressed support for ICC prosecutions in connection with Darfur.

Potential Deferral of the Bashir Prosecution and Security Council Considerations in July 2008: Context and Background

The ICC Prosecutor's request for an arrest warrant for Bashir on July 14, 2008, occurred during the time that the U.N. Security Council was considering extension of the Council mandate for the African Union-United Nations Hybrid Operation in Darfur (UNAMID). The Council had before it the report of the U.N. Secretary-General on the deployment of the operation, dated July 7 and covering the period April to June 2008.[89] It was expected that this mandate, which was to expire July 31, would be extended, albeit with some discussion of UNAMID-related issues.

Council considerations were significantly impacted by the ICC Prosecutor's announcement. In the light of reactions to this request (see previous section) and in view of the fact that the Council had sent the case to the ICC for investigation, protracted consultations within the Council on the content of a resolution extending the UNAMID mandate delayed Council action until nearly the final hour.[90]

Among the issues engaging Council members after the July 14 action was the oft-made suggestion that the Council include in its resolution a request, under Article 16 of the ICC Statute, for a deferral or suspension of further ICC action on the case for up to 12 months for the purpose of, among other things, facilitating efforts toward a peaceful settlement of the situations in Darfur and south Sudan. Some governments also expressed concerns that a positive ICC response to the request for an arrest warrant would exacerbate the situation on the ground in Darfur, making both peacekeepers and humanitarian workers subject to further attacks.

> No investigation or prosecution can be commenced or proceeded with under this Statute for a period of 12 months after the Security Council, in a resolution adopted under Chapter VII of the Charter of the United Nations, has requested the Court to that effect; that request may be renewed by the Council under the same conditions.

Thus, if the U.N. Security Council, acting under Chapter VII of the Charter, adopts a resolution requesting the ICC to suspend or defer any further investigation or prosecution of the case against Bashir, the ICC, including the Prosecutor, would be obliged to cease its investigation in that particular situation and the Pre-Trial Chamber, before which the warrant request is pending, would have to suspend its considerations. The Council request would be applicable for 12 months and would be renewable.

David Scheffer, who headed the U.S. delegation to the conference that drafted the ICC Statute, in an August 20, 2008, Op-ed in *Jurist*, noted that the "negotiating history of Article 16 should be instructive to how the Council currently examines the Darfur situation."[91] Scheffer alleged that Article 16 was drafted and adopted to enable the U.N. Security Council to suspend or defer an ICC investigation or prosecution of a situation "*before either is launched* if priorities of peace and security compelled a delay of international justice." He stated that "the original intent behind Article 16 was for the Security Council to act pre-emptively to delay the application of international justice for atrocity crimes in a particular situation in order to focus exclusively on performing the Council's mandated responsibilities for international peace and security objectives." This was a tool to be employed by the Council in instances of "premature State Party or Prosecutor referrals." In addition, Scheffer claimed that if the current proposals for Council suspension of further ICC action on a situation referred to the ICC by the Council had been foreseen, "Article 16 never would have been approved by the ... majority of governments attending the U.N. talks on the Rome Statute for it would have been viewed as creating rights for the Security Council far beyond the original intent of the Singapore compromise."

Scheffer noted, "Nonetheless, one plausibly may argue that the language of Article 16 of the Rome Statute technically empowers the Security Council to intervene at this late date and block approval of an arrest warrant against President Bashir or even suspend its execution following any approval of it by the judges."[92]

U.N. Security Council Resolution 1828 (2008), adopted on July 31, 2008, by a vote of 14 in favor and with the United States abstaining, extended

UNAMID for a further 12 months.[93] In abstaining on the vote rather than voting against it, the United States supported renewal of the UNAMID mandate but noted that the language in preambular paragraph 9 "would send the wrong signal to President Bashir and undermine efforts to bring him and others to justice."[94] In remarks with the press following the vote, U.S. Deputy Permanent Representative Alejandro Wolff stated:

> The reason for our abstention ... had to do with one paragraph that would send the wrong signal at a very important time when we are trying to eliminate the climate of impunity, to deal with justice, and to address crimes in Darfur, by suggesting that there might be a way out. There is no compromise on the issue of justice. The ... United States felt it was time to stand up on this point of moral clarity and make clear that this Permanent Member of the Security Council will not compromise on the issue of justice.[95]

The United States also abstained on Council Resolution 1828 (2008), extending the UNAMID mandate, pointing to the language in a preambular paragraph that referred to the July 14 application by the ICC prosecutor and the possibility of a Council request for deferral of further consideration of ICC consideration of that case as the reason for the abstention. While the Bush Administration would have likely preferred a different venue for consideration of the genocide conditions in Darfur, it did not halt referral to the ICC by vetoing the resolution.

Some observers have suggested that the U.S. position in the past would not have permitted abstention on the two Council resolutions. Thus, they maintain that under the Bush Administration, the United States moved to a policy that recognized that under certain circumstances, the ICC might have a role.[96] Others have pointed out, however, that any perceived moderation in U.S. views toward the Court did not affect its overall position not to become a party to the ICC Statute.

The two U.S. abstentions in the Council appear to have been driven by non-ICC foreign policy issues that were perceived as more important. The need to support the U.S. policy against genocide in Darfur was perceived as more important than overall U.S. opposition to the ICC. (This broader policy drove the U.S. abstention on Council referral of the situation to the ICC in 2005.) Moreover, the need to ensure that the UNAMID mandate, on the brink of expiring, was extended for another 12 months was also perceived as more important and led to the U.S. abstention in July 2008.

Uganda: The Lord's Resistance Army

The government of Uganda, a party to the ICC, referred "the situation concerning the Lord's Resistance Army" to the ICC in 2003.[97] The Lord's Resistance Army (LRA) is a rebel group that has fought for over two decades in northern Uganda.[98] In October 2005, the ICC unsealed arrest warrants—the first issued by the Court—for LRA leader Joseph Kony and commanders Vincent Otti, Okot Odhiambo, Dominic Ongwen, and Raska Lukwiya. The Prosecutor accused the LRA of establishing "a pattern of brutalization of civilians," including murder, forced abduction, sexual enslavement, and mutilation, amounting to crimes against humanity and war crimes.[99] None of the suspects are in custody. Lukwiya and Otti have reportedly been killed since the warrants were issued, while other LRA commanders are thought to be in neighboring countries. The Prosecutor is also reportedly investigating actions by the Ugandan military in northern Uganda.

Although LRA atrocities have been widely documented, ICC actions in Uganda have met with some domestic and international opposition due to debates over what would constitute justice for the war-torn communities of northern Uganda and whether the ICC has helped or hindered the pursuit of a peace agreement.[100] Some observers argue that ICC arrest warrants were a crucial factor in bringing the LRA to the negotiating table in 2006 for peace talks brokered by the Government of South Sudan. In August 2006, rebel and government representatives signed a landmark cessation of hostilities agreement; in February 2008, the government and the LRA reached several significant further agreements, including a permanent cease-fire. However, the LRA has demanded that ICC arrest warrants be annulled as a prerequisite to a final agreement, and threats of ICC prosecution are considered by many to be a stumbling block to achieving an elusive final peace deal.

The Ugandan government has offered a combination of amnesty and domestic prosecutions for lower-and mid-ranking LRA fighters, and is reportedly willing to prosecute LRA leaders in domestic courts if the rebels accept a peace agreement.[101] In March 2010, the Ugandan parliament passed legislation known as the International Criminal Court Bill, which creates provisions in Ugandan law for the punishment of genocide, crimes against humanity, and war crimes. Ugandan attempts to prosecute the LRA leaders domestically could entail challenging the LRA cases' admissibility before the ICC under the principle of complementarity; however, only the ICC's Pre-Trial Chamber has the authority to make a decision on admissibility, and only the ICC Prosecutor can move to drop the case.[102]

Democratic Republic of Congo (DRC)

The DRC government referred "the situation of crimes within the jurisdiction of the Court allegedly committed anywhere in the territory of the DRC" to the Prosecutor in April 2004.[103] Despite the end of a five-year civil war in 2003 and the holding of national elections in 2006, DRC continues to suffer from armed conflict, particularly in the volatile eastern regions bordering Rwanda, Uganda, and Burundi. The ICC has issued four arrest warrants in its first DRC investigation, which focuses on the eastern Congolese district of Ituri, where an inter-ethnic war erupted in June 2003 with reported involvement by neighboring governments.[104] Three suspects are in custody, while a fourth remains at large. A second investigation focuses on sexual crimes and other abuses committed in the eastern provinces of North and South Kivu. One case has been made public in connection with the Kivus investigation; the suspect was arrested in France in October 2010.

Thomas Lubanga Dyilo

The ICC issued a sealed arrest warrant in February 2006 for Thomas Lubanga Dyilo, the alleged founder and leader of the Union of Congolese Patriots (UPC, after its French acronym) in Ituri and its military wing, the Patriotic Forces for the Liberation of Congo (FPLC). At the time, Lubanga was in Congolese custody and had been charged in the domestic justice system.[105] After a determination of admissibility by the ICC, Lubanga was transferred to ICC custody in March 2006. The ICC has charged Lubanga with three counts of war crimes related to the recruitment and use of child soldiers.[106] Following a lengthy delay due to a procedural challenge, Lubanga's trial began in January 2009.

Lubanga has pleaded not guilty: his defense team maintains that Lubanga was only a political leader who tried to demobilize children fighting in his group, and that he is a scapegoat for other, more senior militant leaders.[107] The trial has been beset by procedural challenges. Judges have twice halted proceedings and ordered Lubanga's release (most recently, in July 2010), contending that a fair trial was impossible because prosecutors had erred in handling evidence and refused to disclose sources' identities to judges and the defense. In each instance, prosecutors successfully appealed to overturn the judges' decision, allowing the trial to resume.[108]

Germain Katanga and Mathieu Ngudjolo Chui

Germain Katanga, the alleged commander of the *Force de Rsistance Patriotique en Ituri* (FRPI) and Ngudjolo, the alleged highest-ranking commander of the *Front des Nationalistes et Intgrationnistes* (FNI), are being prosecuted as co-perpetrators for allegedly having "acted in concert to mount an attack targeted mainly at Hema civilians" in Ituri in 2003.[109] The ICC issued sealed arrest warrants for Katanga and Ngudjolo in July 2007, and they were transferred by Congolese authorities to ICC custody in October 2007 and February 2008, respectively. The Prosecutor has accused them jointly of four counts of crimes against humanity and nine counts of war crimes related to murder, "inhumane acts," sexual crimes, the use of child soldiers, rape, and other abuses.[110] In November 2009, the joint trial of Katanga and Ngudjolo opened.

Bosco Ntaganda

The ICC issued a sealed warrant for the arrest of Bosco Ntaganda, the alleged former deputy military commander in Lubanga's FPLC militia, in August 2006. The warrant was unsealed in April 2008, but Ntaganda remains at large. Ntaganda is accused of three counts of war crimes related to the recruitment and use of child soldiers in 2002 and 2003.[111] His nationality is disputed: the ICC arrest warrant states that he is "believed to be a Rwandan national," but other sources state that he is an ethnic Tutsi from DRC's North Kivu province.[112]

At the time the warrant was unsealed, Ntaganda was a commander in a different rebel group, the National Congress for the People's Defense (CNDP), in North Kivu. Ntaganda later agreed to be integrated into the Congolese armed forces as part of a January 2009 peace deal, and he was reportedly promoted to the rank of military general. The Congolese government has since refused to pursue Ntaganda on behalf of the ICC, arguing that to do so would jeopardize peace efforts in the Kivu region.[113] Foreign diplomats and human rights advocates allege that Ntaganda is living openly in the North Kivu city of Goma; that he has played a command role in a high-profile DRC military offensive in the east since early 2009, contrary to statements by the U.N. peacekeeping mission in Congo, which supported the offensive; and that he has continued to orchestrate extrajudicial killings and disappearances of perceived opponents.[114] Others have alleged that he is involved in illicit minerals smuggling.[115] In November 2009, the Obama Administration's then-Special Advisor on the Great Lakes Region, Howard Wolpe, stated that the DRC's protection of Ntaganda was "inexcusable" and said that the United

States would press Congolese authorities to allow Ntaganda's transfer to the ICC.

Callixte Mbarushimana

ICC judges issued a sealed warrant for the arrest of Callixte Mbarushimana, a Rwandan national and the alleged political leader in exile of the Democratic Forces for the Liberation of Rwanda (FDLR) militia, on September 28, 2010. The warrant cites "reasonable grounds" to believe Mbarushimana is criminally responsible for six counts of war crimes and five counts of crimes against humanity.[116] On October 12, Mbarushimana was arrested in France, where he was living as a political refugee. A French court verdict on November 3 paved the way for his transfer to ICC custody on January 25, 2011.

The FDLR is based in the conflict-ridden Kivu provinces of eastern DRC but is primarily led by Rwandan Hutu extremists, including individuals who fled to DRC during the aftermath of the 1994 Rwandan genocide as well as members of the diaspora.[117] The Prosecutor's case against Mbarushimana alleges that he commanded FDLR attacks against civilians in the Kivus, including murder, torture, rape, and the destruction of property. The United States welcomed the arrest, noting that Mbarushimana has been the target of U.N. and U.S. sanctions since 2008, and indicating U.S. support for the ICC's "ongoing investigations into atrocities that have been committed in the Democratic Republic of the Congo."[118]

Central African Republic (CAR)

The government of CAR, a party to the ICC, referred "the situation of crimes within the jurisdiction of the Court committed anywhere on [CAR] territory" to the ICC Prosecutor in January 2005.[119]

Jean-Pierre Bemba Gombo

In May 2008, the ICC issued a sealed warrant of arrest for Jean-Pierre Bemba Gombo. A former DRC rebel leader turned politician and successful businessman, Bemba had been the leading challenger to incumbent President Joseph Kabila in DRC's 2006 presidential election, and was elected to the Congolese legislature in January 2007. He subsequently went into exile in Europe following armed clashes with security forces loyal to Kabila. The warrant alleged that as commander of the Movement for the Liberation of Congo (MLC), one of two main DRC rebel groups during that country's civil war (1998-2003), Bemba had overseen systematic attacks on civilians in CAR territory between October 2002 and March 2003. Bemba's MLC, based in the DRC's north, allegedly committed these abuses after it was invited into CAR by then-President Ange-Félix Patassé to help quell a rebellion.[120]

Bemba was arrested in Belgium in May 2008 and turned over to the ICC in July 2008. In June 2009, a panel of ICC judges confirmed three charges of war crimes and two charges of crimes against humanity for alleged rape, murder, and pillaging.[121] The charges hinge on the question of command responsibility: the Prosecutor contends that Bemba personally managed the MLC, stayed in constant contact with combatants, and was well informed about the group's activities in CAR.[122] Bemba's trial opened on November 22, 2010, after ICC judges dismissed various legal appeals. The prosecution has been controversial in the DRC, where Bemba's MLC continues to function as an opposition party. The Office of the Prosecutor has denied that political considerations played a role in the case, and the government of DRC has denied involvement in the prosecution.[123]

Issues Raised by the ICC's Actions in Africa

Some observers have praised the ICC's investigations in Africa as a crucial step against impunity on the continent, but ICC actions have also provoked debates over the court's potential impact, its perceived prioritization of Africa over other regions, its selection of cases, and the potential effect of prosecutions on peace processes. Notably, critics have accused the ICC of potentially jeopardizing political settlements that may keep the peace in the pursuit of an often abstract "justice." Supporters of the Court reject these criticisms, and hope that ICC investigations will contribute to Africa's long-term peace and stability.

Impact on Deterrence

The ICC's founders anticipated that by ending impunity, the ICC would deter future atrocities.[124] Indeed, some observers argue that the ICC's success should be evaluated not just based on the punishment of past atrocities, but also in terms of "the effect its investigations have on reducing abysmal conduct in the present and future."[125] (The Office of the Prosecutor maintains that the choice of cases is not based on calculations of deterrent effect, though the Office acknowledges that strategic communications related to ICC prosecutions may play a role in deterrence.[126])

The goal of deterrence has been particularly salient in the ICC's investigations in Africa, which have focused on regions where atrocities are ongoing or have only recently ended.[127] However, difficulties encountered in enforcing ICC arrest warrants and the fact that the Court has yet to convict any suspects have led some to question whether the threat of ICC prosecution is credible. Some observers suggest that the Court's failure to apprehend suspects in Sudan, in particular, has bared tensions between the ICC's universal mandate and its reliance on the enforcement power of states.[128] Others maintain that deterrence is difficult to evaluate and that changes in perpetrators' behavior may be visible only over the long run. Some argue that the Court's compilation of evidence, including transcribed interviews with witnesses, may serve future prosecutions or reconciliation processes even if they do not immediately lead to convictions.

Accusations of Bias

The ICC's investigations in Africa have stirred concerns over African sovereignty, in part due to the long history of foreign intervention on the continent. For example, President Paul Kagame of Rwanda, a country which is not a party to the Court, has portrayed the ICC as a form of "imperialism" that seeks to "undermine people from poor and African countries, and other powerless countries in terms of economic development and politics."[129] Some commentators allege that the Prosecutor has limited investigations to Africa because of geopolitical pressures, either out of a desire to avoid confrontation with major powers or as a tool of Western foreign policy.[130] The attempt to prosecute Bashir has been particularly controversial, drawing rebuke from African governments and regional organizations. Jean Ping, president of the AU Commission, has accused the ICC of hypocrisy, contending that "we are not against the ICC, but there are two systems of measurement ... the ICC seems to exist solely for judging Africans."[131]

Supporters of the Court respond that most investigations to-date have been determined by referrals, either by African states or the Security Council, and that the Prosecutor continues to analyze situations outside of Africa. The

Office of the Prosecutor maintains that its choice of cases is based on the relative gravity of abuses, and that crimes committed in Sub-Saharan Africa are among the world's most serious.[132] A prominent South African jurist, Constitutional Court Chief Justice Sandile Ngcobo, recently expressed a similar interpretation, stating that "abuses committed in Sub-Saharan Africa have been among the most serious, and this is certainly a legitimate criterion for the selection of cases."[133]

Supporters also contend that national legal systems in Africa are particularly weak, which has allowed the ICC to assert its jurisdiction under the principle of complementarity.[134] These sentiments were echoed by former U.N. Secretary-General Kofi Annan, who stated, "In all of these cases, it is the culture of impunity, not African countries, which are the target. This is exactly the role of the I.C.C. It is a court of last resort."[135] At the June 2010 meeting of ICC states parties in Kampala, Uganda, participants initiated mechanisms for increasing coordination between donors on strengthening national justice systems. The United States, which participated in the meeting as an observer, has expressed support for such efforts.[136]

The Prosecutor's selection of cases also has proven controversial. As one pair of authors has written, "perceptions of the ICC on the ground have at times been damaged by insufficient efforts by the Court to make clear the basis on which individuals have been the subject of warrants and of particular charges, while those of apparently equal culpability have not."[137] For example, some have criticized ICC prosecutions in Uganda, the DRC, and CAR for focusing on alleged abuses by rebel fighters to the exclusion of those reportedly committed by government troops.[138] The decision to pursue DRC opposition leader Jean-Pierre Bemba Gombo has provoked accusations that the Prosecutor was swayed by political bias or, potentially, excessive pragmatism, since other Congolese and CAR politicians accused of similar abuses have not been pursued to date. ICC supporters have responded that the Prosecutor is mandated to focus on particularly serious cases, and that investigations are ongoing in these countries.

Justice vs. Peace?

One of the most persistent criticisms of the ICC's actions in Africa has been that by prosecuting participants in ongoing or recently settled conflicts, the Court risks prolonging violence or endangering fragile peace processes. By removing the bargaining chip of amnesty from the negotiating table, critics allege, the ICC may remove incentives for peace settlements while encouraging perpetrators to remain in power in order to shield themselves from prosecution. Some analysts observe that in such cases, "it is difficult to tell victims of these conflicts that the prosecution of a small number of people should take precedence over a peace deal that may end the appalling conditions they endure and the daily risks they face."[139]

Concerns that the aims of "justice" and "peace" may conflict have been particularly prominent in connection with the Lord's Resistance Army, Darfur, and—more recently—Kenya. Some argue that ICC arrest warrants against LRA commanders acted as an impediment to achieving a final peace agreement to that long-running conflict. Ugandan critics include community elders who support the use of traditional reconciliation mechanisms instead of international prosecution.[140] Conversely, others contend that the threat of ICC prosecution could serve as "an important ingredient in a political solution" for the conflict-plagued north.[141] This discussion has been muted in recent years, as senior LRA commanders are no longer in northern Uganda and have sought refuge instead in neighboring countries. In Sudan, some observers have argued that the attempt to prosecute President Bashir could endanger the Comprehensive Peace Agreement for Southern Sudan and the peace process in Darfur, or provide an incentive to the ruling party to cling to power. For example, according to former U.S. special envoy to Sudan Andrew Natsios, "the regime will now avoid any compromise or anything that would weaken their already weakened position, because if they are forced from office they face trials before the ICC.... [An ICC warrant for Bashir] may well shut off the last remaining hope for a peaceful settlement for the country."[142] In Kenya, concerns persist that ICC prosecutions could destabilize the fragile political truce that has underpinned the post-2007 government of national unity, although some argue that a lack of accountability for human rights violations would also threaten future stability.

Criticisms connected to the case against Bashir in Sudan were reinforced when the Sudanese government responded to the ICC arrest warrant for Bashir by expelling aid agencies and threatening NGOs and peacekeeping troops. In March 2009 testimony before Congress, when asked about the impact of the ICC warrant on U.N. peacekeeping operations in Darfur, then-Director of National Intelligence Dennis C. Blair said that "the indictment and President Bashir's reaction have made him less cooperative than he was" and that the warrant would "make it harder" for peacekeeping operations in Darfur.[143] In early August 2009, the outgoing commander of the hybrid U.N.-AU peacekeeping mission in Darfur (UNAMID), General Martin Luther Agwai, reportedly stated that the decision to pursue Bashir had been a "big blow" for UNAMID and the peace process, although it had not had as drastic an effect on the ground as he had feared.[144] U.N. Secretary-General Ban Ki-moon, who has maintained a neutral position on the ICC's actions in Sudan, has nonetheless argued that the international community must seek to balance "peace" and "justice" in dealing with the conflict in Darfur and expressed concern that the expulsion of aid organizations was detrimental to relief and peacekeeping operations.[145]

Supporters of the Court maintain that the warrant against Bashir may open up new opportunities to secure peace in Darfur, as a credible threat of prosecution may serve as an important lever of pressure on actors in a conflict.[146] For example, Priscilla Hayner of the International Center for Transitional Justice has written that "it would be wrong to suggest that pragmatism always trumps principle in matters of life and death, and thus that one must ease up on justice in order to achieve peace. In some cases, the interest of peace has been well served by strong, forthright efforts to advance justice."[147] Some argue that "peace deals that sacrifice justice often fail to produce peace" in the long run.[148] Many observers point out that discerning the effect of ICC actions on complex processes is extremely difficult.

Appendix. African States that are ICC Parties and Have Concluded an "Article 98 Agreement" with the United States

Country	Party to ICC	Ratified Article 98 Agreement
Algeria		X
Angola		X
Benin	X	X
Botswana	X	X
Burkina Faso	X	X
Burundi	X	X
Cameroon		X
Cape Verde		X
Central African Republic	X	X
Chad	X	X
Comoros	X	X
Congo, Republic of	X	X
Congo, Democratic	X	X

Country	Party to ICC	Ratified Article 98 Agreement
Republic of Côte d'Ivoire		X
Djibouti	X	X
Egypt		X
Equatorial Guinea		X
Eritrea		X
Ethiopia		
Gabon	X	X
Gambia, The	X	X
Ghana	X	X
Guinea	X	X
Guinea-Bissau		X
Kenya	X	
Lesotho	X	X
Liberia	X	X
Libya		
Madagascar	X	X
Malawi	X	X
Mali	X	
Mauritania		X
Mauritius	X	X
Morocco		X
Mozambique Namibia	X	X
NigerNigeria Rwanda	X	X
	X	X
São Tomé and Príncipe		X
SenegalSeychelles		X
Sierra Leone	X	X
	X	X
Somalia		
South Africa	X	
Sudan		
Swaziland		X
Tanzania	X	
Togo Tunisia		X X
UgandaZambia	X X	X X
Zimbabwe		

Sources: United Nations, Multilateral Treaties Deposited with the Secretary-General; U.S. Department of State, Treaties in Force 2007.

In: International Criminal Court
Editor: Michael N. Baker
ISBN: 978-1-61324-694-8

Chapter 3

THE INTERNATIONAL CRIMINAL COURT (ICC): JURISDICTION, EXTRADITION AND U.S. POLICY*

Emily C. Barbour and Matthew C. Weed

SUMMARY

The International Criminal Court (ICC) is the first permanent international court with jurisdiction to prosecute individuals for "the most serious crimes of concern to the international community." Currently, 110 countries are States Parties to the ICC. Since its inception in 2002, the ICC has received three referrals for investigations by States Parties and one referral from the United Nations Security Council.

While the U.S. executive branch initially supported the idea of creating an international criminal court, the United States ultimately voted against the Statute of the ICC (the "Rome Statute") and informed the United Nations that the United States did not intend to become a State Party to the Rome Statute. The United States' primary objection to the treaty has been the potential for the ICC to assert jurisdiction over U.S. civilian policymakers and U.S. soldiers charged with "war crimes."

This concern has been highlighted with recent preliminary investigations by the ICC's Prosecutor into alleged war crimes in the

* This is an edited, reformatted and augmented version of a Congressional Research Service 7-5700, www.crs.gov, R41116 publication, Prepared for Members and Committees of Congress, dated March 16, 2010.

Middle East and Afghanistan. In 2006, the ICC's Office of the Prosecutor completed a preliminary investigation into alleged war crimes in Iraq, finding that the information did not establish sufficient grounds for the Prosecutor to launch a formal investigation into the situation. In 2009, the Office of the Prosecutor confirmed that it was conducting another preliminary investigation into possible war crimes committed by NATO soldiers, U.S. soldiers, and both Taliban and al Qaeda insurgents in Afghanistan. That same year, the Palestinian National Authority (PNA) sought the ICC's jurisdiction over alleged crimes committed during the Gaza conflict of December 2008/January 2009, and the United Nations Commission of Inquiry on Gaza issued a report recommending that the Security Council refer the situation to the ICC Prosecutor if Israel and the PNA did not undertake appropriate national level investigations and prosecutions.

The United States has taken both diplomatic and domestic actions with the potential to affect the ICC's authority over U.S. citizens. On a diplomatic level, the United States has concluded bilateral immunity agreements (BIAs) with many ICC States Parties to prevent other countries from surrendering U.S. citizens to the ICC without U.S. consent under Article 98 of the Rome Statute. These agreements have generated a vigorous debate over when and whether obligations in international agreements preempt an ICC request to a State Party for the arrest and surrender of a person in its territory. However, the ICC, in which the Rome Statute vests the sole responsibility for interpreting the Statute's text, has remained silent on the question, neither validating nor refuting the U.S. position that BIAs or any agreement creating similar obligations preempt an ICC request to surrender.

Although remaining opposed to U.S. ratification of the Rome Statute, the Bush Administration in its second term took actions that suggested its support for some ICC activities. The Obama Administration has also taken a more supportive stance towards the ICC and has begun to engage directly with the Court. The Obama Administration is currently reviewing its ICC policy and is expected to announce its conclusions sometime in 2010. Similarly, actions by Congress have eliminated or chosen not to extend provisions affecting U.S. assistance for countries that are ICC States Parties. Although these actions seem to soften Congress's position on the ICC, the changes might also be interpreted as a decision to reverse sanctions that were perceived as hurting U.S. interests.

INTRODUCTION

The International Criminal Court ("ICC" or "Court") is the first permanent international court with jurisdiction to prosecute individuals for "the most serious crimes of concern to the international community."[1] It sits at The Hague in the Netherlands but may hold proceedings anywhere in the world. It is funded primarily by States Parties. The Statute of the International Criminal Court (the "Rome Statute" or "Statute"), which created the ICC, established ICC jurisdiction over persons who, following the Statute's entry into force on July 1, 2002, commit certain offenses.[2] One hundred and ten countries, not including the United States, are States Parties to the ICC.

Since its inception, the ICC has received referrals for investigations from three States Parties[3] and one referral from the United Nations Security Council.[4] After receiving referrals, the Chief Prosecutor carries out a preliminary analysis to determine whether to initiate an investigation. The Chief Prosecutor opened investigations into all four of these referred cases.[5] Additionally, in November 2009, the Prosecutor of the ICC requested authorization to investigate alleged postelection crimes in Kenya without a referral.[6] This marked the first time that the ICC Prosecutor has sought to open an investigation on his own initiative instead of by referral. To date, the Court has issued 12 arrest warrants, four of which have resulted in actual arrests.[7] The ICC currently has nine cases before it, although some of the defendants in these cases remain at large.[8] The ICC Prosecutor has also announced preliminary, but not formal, investigations into situations in Palestine and Afghanistan, both of which were ongoing at the date of this report's publication.

The Court may impose a period of imprisonment on persons convicted under the Rome Statute as well as a fine and forfeiture of proceeds, property, and other assets derived from the crime.[9] This report focuses first on the process by which the Office of the Prosecutor investigates allegations of war crimes and second on U.S policy towards the ICC. In particular, this report seeks to address the concern that the ICC might assert jurisdiction over U.S. nationals by providing insight into (1) how the ICC and Prosecutor determine whether the ICC has jurisdiction over the situations under preliminary investigation; (2) how the Prosecutor and ICC determine whether a situation would be admissible as a case before the ICC; (3) the basis for concerns that the ICC has the authority to request the surrender of a U.S. national; and (4) steps taken by the United States to prevent or deter the ICC from exercising jurisdiction over U.S. nationals.

THE HISTORY OF U.S. POLICY TOWARD THE ICC

While the U.S. executive branch initially supported the idea of creating an international criminal court[10] and was a major participant at the United Nations Conference of Plenipotentiaries on the Establishment of an International Criminal Court ("Rome Conference"), which produced the Statute,[11] the United States ultimately voted against the Statute.[12] President Clinton signed the treaty at the close of 2000 but declared that it contained "significant flaws" and would not be submitted to the Senate for ratification "until our fundamental concerns are satisfied."[13] The United States stated that its primary objection to the treaty is the potential for the ICC to assert jurisdiction over both U.S. civilian policymakers and U.S. soldiers charged with "war crimes" even if the United States does not ratify the Rome Statute.

Following the Rome Statute's entry into force in 2002, both President George W. Bush's Administration and the U.S. Congress took several steps to weaken the ICC's potential effect on U.S. citizens. First, the Bush Administration "unsigned" the Rome Statute by informing the United Nations that the United States did not intend to become a party to the Rome Statute.[14] This action released the United States from its treaty obligation to refrain from undermining the Rome Statute and enabled both Congress and the executive branch to take actions that could be perceived as undercutting the Rome Statute. Additionally, the United States secured a U.N. Security Council resolution deferring any potential ICC prosecution of U.S. personnel involved in international peacekeeping missions; concluded bilateral immunity agreements to prevent the ICC from being able to exercise jurisdiction over U.S. nationals; and enacted the American Servicemembers' Protection Act. A detailed explanation of each action is provided below.

U.S. Diplomatic Actions Affecting the ICC

Concerned that U.S. participation in international peacekeeping would be imperiled if U.S. soldiers and employees were subject to ICC jurisdiction,[15] the United States reportedly threatened to veto a draft U.N. Security Council resolution to extend the peacekeeping mission in Bosnia and Herzegovina unless U.S. personnel were granted full immunity from the jurisdiction of the ICC.[16] Ultimately, the Security Council and the U.S. delegation compromised, adopting a resolution asking the ICC to defer, for an initial period of one year, any prosecution of persons who are both (1) participants in U.N.-established or authorized operations and (2) nationals of States not party to the Rome Statute.[17] The resulting resolution did not provide permanent immunity for U.S. soldiers and officials from prosecution by the ICC, but, in conjunction with Article 16 of the Rome Statute, it deferred potential prosecutions of U.S. soldiers and officials for one year.[18] Some criticized the resolution as a misapplication of Article 16, arguing that Article 16 was meant to apply only to specific *cases*, not to permit a blanket waiver for citizens of specific *countries*.

Nevertheless, in a resolution adopted in 2003, the U.N. Security Council extended the deferral to July 1, 2004.[19] By 2005, however, sufficient opposition to the resolution had developed to deter the Bush Administration from seeking another extension. Consequently, the resolution expired, and the Security Council has not taken any action since to defer potential ICC prosecutions of American soldiers engaged in U.N. established or authorized operations.

In the wake of "unsigning" of the Rome Statute, the United States also began concluding bilateral immunity agreements (BIAs), which contain promises by one or both parties that no surrender of citizens of the other signatory would be made to the ICC absent both parties' consent.[20] These agreements are intended to fall within the provisions of Article 98 of the Rome Statute, which serve to limit the duty to surrender individuals to the ICC under circumstances where such surrender would force a country to violate its obligations under (1) international law concerning diplomatic immunity or (2) certain international agreements with another country. These BIAs provide that a contracting country may not surrender U.S. military personnel, as well as a number of other types of U.S. persons (including in many cases all U.S. nationals), to the ICC. The provisions are intended to create an obligation under an international agreement that would supersede the non-U.S. party's obligations under the Rome Statute to hand over suspects to the ICC, pursuant to Article 98.[21] The U.S. has occasionally used sanctions to induce countries to enter these BIAs.[22]

The American Servicemembers' Protection Act of 2002

On August 2, 2002, President George W. Bush signed the American Servicemembers' Protection Act of 2002 (ASPA) into law (Title II of P.L.

107-206; 22 U.S.C. §§ 7421-7433). This act was designed to provide protections for members of the U.S. armed forces and certain other persons from ICC prosecution and detention or imprisonment arising therefrom. It generally prohibits U.S. government cooperation with the ICC by (1) restricting the use of appropriated funds to assist the ICC;[23] (2) restricting U.S. participation in certain U.N. peacekeeping operations due to possible ICC prosecution; and (3) authorizing the President to free members of the U.S. armed forces and other individuals detained or imprisoned by or on behalf of the ICC. Section 2015 of the act (22 U.S.C. § 7433) created an exception from the prohibition on assisting the ICC for assistance to bring to justice foreign nationals accused of genocide, war crimes, or crimes against humanity.[24] Until it was repealed under P.L. 110-181, Section 2007 of ASPA prohibited providing U.S. military assistance to ICC States Parties. Provisions enacted in the 2005, 2006, and 2008 Foreign Operations Appropriations bills (so-called "Nethercutt Amendment" provisions) contained similar funding prohibitions for Economic Support Fund (ESF) assistance to ICC States Parties.[25]

Current Attitudes

Despite its early objections to the Rome State, the Bush Administration in its second term took actions that seemed to show acceptance of some ICC activities.[26] The Obama Administration seems to have continued this approach and has started engaging directly with the ICC.[27] Similarly, recent actions by Congress have eliminated sanctions provisions affecting U.S. assistance for countries that are ICC members.

The International Criminal Court's Jurisdiction

Article 12: Preconditions to the Exercise of Jurisdiction

The ICC is a treaty-based court, which means countries can decide whether to become a party to the Rome Statute.[28] As a result, the Court does not have universal jurisdiction.[29] Instead, the ICC can only exercise jurisdiction over crimes that were either (1) committed on the territory of a country that has accepted the ICC's jurisdiction; (2) committed by nationals of a country that has accepted jurisdiction; or (3) referred to the ICC by the United Nations Security Council.[30] The only exception to this rule permits ICC jurisdiction over situations when both (1) a non-State Party has accepted the exercise of jurisdiction by the ICC with respect to the crime in question; and (2) the alleged crime either took place in the consenting country's territory or was committed by a national of that country.[31] To obtain the Court's ad hoc jurisdiction, the country seeking it must lodge a declaration with the ICC Registrar and cooperate with the Court accordingly.[32]

Article 17: Issues of Admissibility

Even if the ICC has jurisdiction over a case, it may be precluded from hearing it if the case is inadmissible under Article 17, which states:

> the Court shall determine that a case is inadmissible where: (a) The case is being investigated or prosecuted by a State which has jurisdiction over it, unless the State is unwilling or unable genuinely to carry out the investigation or prosecution; (b) The case has been investigated by a State which has jurisdiction over it and the State has decided not to prosecute the person concerned, unless the decision resulted from the unwillingness or inability of the State genuinely to prosecute; (c) The person concerned has already been tried for conduct which is the subject of the complaint, and a trial by the Court is not permitted under article 20, paragraph 3; (d) The case is not of sufficient gravity to justify further action by the Court.33

Once the jurisdiction of the Court is triggered, the Court's interpretation of the applicability of Article 17 to a given case is considered dispositive, at least so far as States Parties are concerned.[34]

Under Article 17, a case is inadmissible if it concerns conduct that is the subject of genuine legal proceedings brought by a country with jurisdiction.[35] The ICC's subordination to the criminal proceedings of sovereign nations is premised upon the principle of complementarity, which enables the ICC to maintain its role as the court of last resort and thereby support State justice systems.[36]

In determining whether complementarity prevents a case from being admitted to the ICC, the Court considers (1) the willingness of the investigating country to pursue "genuine" proceedings, and (2) the ability of that country to effectively investigate and prosecute the suspects. If the ICC feels that the country is either unwilling or unable to investigate, the principle of complementarity does not apply and the case may proceed at the ICC.[37]

To assess a State Party's willingness to investigate and prosecute an alleged crime, the Court conducts a three-part analysis, asking whether (1) the proceedings are being undertaken for the purpose of shielding the person concerned from criminal responsibility for crimes within the jurisdiction of the Court; (2) there has been an unjustified delay in the proceedings which is inconsistent with an intent to bring the person concerned to justice; and (3) the proceedings are being conducted independently or impartially rather than in a manner that is inconsistent with an intent to bring the person concerned to justice.[38] It appears from the case law that the key to this analysis is whether the country acts with good faith in investigating and prosecuting suspected war criminals.[39] This intent can be proved by reference to a country's express statement or, alternatively, it can be "inferred from unambiguous facts."[40]

As for the second factor in complementarity, whether a country has the ability to investigate and prosecute in a particular situation, the Court employs an arguably simpler standard: whether, due to a total or substantial collapse or unavailability of its national judicial system, the country is unable to apprehend the accused, obtain the necessary evidence or testimony, or otherwise carry out its proceedings.[41]

THE OFFICE OF THE PROSECUTOR OF THE ICC

The ICC Office of the Prosecutor (the Office), which is headed by Prosecutor Luis MorenoOcampo, is composed of three divisions: the Prosecutions Division, the Jurisdiction Complementarity and Cooperation Division, and the Investigations Division. The Prosecutor is elected by secret ballot by an absolute majority of the members of the Assembly of States Parties.[42] The Prosecutor must have "high moral character," competence and extensive practical experience in prosecuting or trying criminal cases, and fluency in one of the six working languages of the Court (Arabic, Chinese, English, French, Russian, and Spanish).[43] The Prosecutor holds office for a term of nine years and is not eligible for re-election.[44]

The Office of the Prosecutor is required to act as an independent and separate organ of the Court.[45] It is responsible for (1) receiving referrals about alleged war crimes and any substantiated information on crimes within the jurisdiction of the Court; (2) examining these referrals and conducting investigations; and (3) conducting prosecutions before the Court.[46] The Prosecutor must not participate in any matter in which his impartiality might reasonably be doubted, and he is disqualified from a case if he has previously been involved either in that case before the Court or in a case at the national level involving the person being investigated or prosecuted.[47]

Article 98: Extradition to the ICC

If the ICC Prosecutor decides to prosecute someone, Article 89 of the Rome Statute permits the Court to request the arrest and surrender of that person from *any* country where that person may be found.[48] However, a country that is not a party to the Rome Statute is not mandated to comply with such a request.[49] In addition, Article 98 precludes the ICC from making a request for the surrender of a person when doing so would require the requested country to act inconsistently with its obligations under international law or international agreements.[50] Relying on this language in Article 98, the United States has frequently entered into international agreements, often referred to as bilateral immunity agreements (BIAs) or Article 98 Agreements, with States Parties that create obligations designed to prevent the ICC from proceeding with a request to those States Parties for the surrender of a U.S. citizen. The proliferation of Article 98 Agreements has triggered a vigorous international debate over when and whether Article 98 prevents the ICC from requesting that a State Party arrest and surrender a person in its territory. This section of the report seeks to frame and explain that debate.

The Vienna Convention on the Law of Treaties ("VCLT" or "Vienna Convention")[51] states that a treaty should be interpreted in accordance with the "ordinary meaning to be given to the terms of the treaty in their context and in the light of its object and purpose."[52] However, the debate over the meaning of Article 98 in the context of BIAs suggests that there are conflicting interpretations of the "ordinary terms" of Article 98, and, more specifically, whether Article 98 permits ICC States Parties to enter agreements that protect the citizens of a particular country from being surrendered to the ICC.

According to some, the primary intention behind Article 98, and particularly its second paragraph, which explicitly discusses international agreements,[53] was to preserve certain prototypical provisions of Status of Forces Agreements (SOFAs).[54] SOFAs traditionally contain a guarantee that a nation deploying military forces on foreign soil retains primary criminal jurisdiction over its soldiers unless it consents to local prosecution.[55] Advancing that line of thought, the European Union (EU) has argued that Article 98(2) only protects from ICC interference those international treaty obligations that, like the obligations in traditional SOFAs, give immunity to persons who are present on the territory of a requested State because they have been sent on official business.[56] In addition to the negotiating history of Article 98, the EU also draws support from (1) the Vienna Convention on the Law of Treaties, which obliges countries who have signed or otherwise accepted an international agreement pending ratification or formal approval to refrain from acts that would defeat the object and purpose of that agreement;[57] and (2) the provisions in the Rome Statute that require States Parties to cooperate with and assist the Court.[58] Consequently, the EU has argued that, in deciding whether compliance with a request for surrender would conflict with a country's treaty obligations, the ICC may ignore any international treaty obligations that would prevent a member-country from surrendering a person who was not sent to the requested country on official business.[59] However, this position is potentially complicated by reports that, several years after the Rome Conference, the head of the U.S. delegation claimed the United States had contemplated the development of BIA-type agreements during negotiations on Article 98(2).[60]

A second position advanced by the EU and some scholars contends that Article 98 was only intended to permit States Parties to continue to adhere to obligations imposed by agreements that predated their entry into the ICC.61 The EU maintains that Article 98(2) does not extend to agreements that the requested country entered into after signing the Rome Statute.62 The EU Commission reached this conclusion largely on the grounds that the concern guiding the negotiations on Article 98 was the elimination of any obstacle to ratification that could result from already existing agreements.63 Scholars who support this position have also pointed to language in an earlier draft of the Rome Statute that refers only to existing treaty obligations in its description of when an ICC request might be barred for conflicting with international obligations.64 Critics of this position, on the other hand, argue that Article 98 applies to all agreements, whether pre or post-dating the Rome Statute, because the actual ratified language of Article 98(2) does not contain a limitation regarding the time of the conclusion of the international agreements in question.[65]

The ICC has yet to request the surrender of a U.S. citizen from a State Party that has entered a BIA with the United States. Accordingly, it is unclear whether the Court would interpret Article 98 of the Rome Statute as permitting the ICC to proceed with a request to surrender when the sending State has entered an agreement that forbids it from honoring the request.66 Regardless of international and scholarly opinion as to the proper interpretation of Article 98, the Rome Statute vests the ICC with the ultimate legal authority to interpret the requirements and obligations that the Statute imposes on States Parties.67 However, at least one commentator has suggested that the Court's decision making does not take place in a vacuum, but, rather, may be affected by predictions about the implementation and practicality of its judgments. 68 If this is true, the Court may consider not only the text and history of the Rome Statute, but also non-textual concerns, such as whether a request to surrender in the context of a BIA would be worth the cost of requiring the sending State to upset its relations with another country and the possibility that the sending State might choose not to honor the ICC's request. 69 If considered, these practicalities could weigh in favor of the U.S. position on the purpose and effect of Article 98.

THE PRELIMINARY INVESTIGATION OF A SITUATION

Article 53 of the Rome Statute: Initiation of a Formal Investigation

When the Office of the Prosecutor receives information about potential war crimes, it must take several steps before prosecuting the persons alleged to have committed these offenses. The first is a preliminary investigation, or preliminary analysis, in which the Prosecutor decides whether to launch a formal investigation. The second step is the actual initiation of a formal investigation.

The Office of the Prosecutor must consider three factors before deciding to initiate a formal investigation: (1) whether the available information provides a reasonable basis to believe that a crime within the jurisdiction of the Court has been or is being committed;[70] (2) whether a resulting case would meet Article 17's requirements for complementarity;[71] and (3) whether, given the gravity of the crime and the interests of the victims, there are substantial reasons to believe that an investigation would serve the interests of justice.[72]

In assessing the first factor, whether a reasonable basis exists to believe a crime occurred, the Prosecutor may seek additional information from countries, organs of the United Nations, intergovernmental or non-governmental organizations (NGOs), or other reliable sources that he or she deems appropriate.[73] The Prosecutor may also receive written or oral testimony on the matter.[74] To assess the second factor, whether a potential case satisfies Article 17's complementarity regime, the Prosecutor collects similar information on the initiation and progress of national proceedings.[75]

In assessing the third factor, the gravity of an alleged crime, the ICC has considered both whether an alleged offense falls under the scope of its subject matter jurisdiction, and also whether it satisfies an additional threshold of severity in comparison to the thousands of other crimes over which the ICC may exercise jurisdiction.[76] A key consideration in this comparison is the number of victims resulting from each crime.[77]

Although the Office of the Prosecutor has received a significant number of communications regarding alleged offenses, there have been relatively few occasions when the Office has examined these communications and concluded that the basic requirements for even an intensive preliminary examination have been satisfied.[78] Only if the information provided leads the Prosecutor to conclude that the three requirements (reasonable basis, complementarity, and gravity) are satisfied may he submit a request for authorization of an investigation to the Pre-Trial Chamber.[79] In turn, the Pre-Trial Chamber will grant the Prosecutor's request only if it too concludes that there is a reasonable basis to proceed with an investigation.[80] Where the Prosecutor believes the requirements for an investigation are not satisfied, the Prosecutor will inform those who provided the information of his decision not to initiate an investigation. However, a decision not to investigate a situation does not preclude the Prosecutor from considering further information regarding the same situation in light of new facts or evidence.[81]

Over the course of 2009, the Office of the Prosecutor has publicly acknowledged considering information concerning situations in the Republic of Georgia, Colombia, Afghanistan, Côte D'Ivoire, Palestine, and Guinea.[82] This kind of public acknowledgment is not necessarily the norm: the Office of the Prosecutor does not always announce or even admit when a situation is under analysis.[83] In general, the ICC's Rules of Procedure and Evidence require the Prosecutor to keep the analysis process confidential to preserve the privacy of the senders, the confidentiality of submitted information, and the integrity of the analysis and any resulting investigation.[84] However, Office policy permits the Prosecutor to publicly disclose the reasons for a decision to request, or not to request, an investigation if (1) the situation has warranted intensive analysis; (2) the situation has generated public interest and the fact of the analysis is in the public domain; and (3) the reasons can be provided without risk to the safety, well-being, and privacy of senders.[85]

Notable Examples of Preliminary Analyses by the Prosecutor

The following examples of preliminary analyses undertaken by the Office of the Prosecutor are notable for the interest they garnered in the Untied States. Although not all of these analyses have been completed, to date, none of these analyses has resulted in the initiation of formal investigations or trials.

Iraq

In 2006, the Office of the Prosecutor concluded its preliminary investigation into alleged offenses committed in Iraq.[86] The Prosecutor investigated two different categories of alleged crimes: (1) war crimes and (2) willful killing and inhumane treatment of civilians. The Office of the Prosecutor's published discussion of its analysis is instructive on how the Prosecutor approaches a preliminary analysis in light of the mandate to determine whether there is a reasonable basis to believe the alleged crimes occurred, whether a resulting case would satisfy the complementarity regime, and whether the crimes are sufficiently grave to warrant a case before the ICC.

Jurisdiction

The alleged crimes occurred in Iraq, which is not a State Party of the ICC.[87] Therefore, the Court lacked jurisdiction over offenses by nationals of non-ICC States Parties that were committed on Iraq soil.[88] However, some communications submitted to the Prosecutor argued that nationals of ICC States Parties were accessories to crimes committed by nationals of non-member countries.[89] Consequently, the Office's preliminary analysis focused on whether a formal investigation should be launched into the involvement of States Parties' citizens as accessories to either war crimes or crimes against civilians.[90]

Allegations of War Crimes

In its analysis of war crimes allegedly committed by States Parties' nationals, the Office of the Prosecutor reviewed submitted communications, identified those containing substantiated information, examined relevant documentation and video-records, and purportedly conducted an exhaustive search of readily available open source information.[91] Some of the readily available open source information used was from non-governmental organizations including Amnesty International, Human Rights Watch, Iraq Body Count, and Spanish Brigades Against the War in Iraq.[92] The Office also stated that it sought and received additional information on the alleged crimes from other relevant countries and entities.[93]

The Office paid particularly close attention to allegations concerning the targeting of civilians or "clearly excessive" attacks.[94] In that context, a war crime, as defined by the Rome Statute, only occurs if there is an intentional attack directed against civilians or an attack is launched on a military objective with the knowledge that incidental civilian injuries would clearly be excessive relative to the anticipated military advantage.[95] The Office found that the available information established that a considerable number of civilians died or were injured during military operations.[96] However, it believed that the information failed to either sufficiently prove or disprove that (1) there were any *intentional* attacks on civilians; (2) the attacks were clearly excessive in relation to military objectives; and (3) nationals of States Parties were involved in the attacks.[97] These gaps in intelligence led the Office to seek out still more information about the alleged crimes.[98]

Additional information provided by the United Kingdom stated that lists of potential targets were identified in advance; commanders were aware of the need to comply with international humanitarian law; detailed computer modeling was used in assessing targets; target approval was subject to political and legal oversight; and collateral damage assessments were sent back to headquarters.[99] In addition, the United Kingdom claimed that nearly 85% of the weapons released by U.K. aircraft were precision-guided, which, to the Prosecutor, evinced an intent to minimize casualties.[100]

The Office continued to examine several incidents in detail until it felt it had exhausted all measures "appropriate during the analysis phase." [101] Ultimately, the Prosecutor concluded that the available information did not provide a reasonable basis to believe that a crime within the jurisdiction of the Court had been committed.[102] The Prosecutor noted, however, that many facts remained undetermined and its conclusion could be reviewed in light of new facts or evidence.[103]

Allegations of Willful Killing and Inhumane Treatment

After allegations came to light in media reports concerning incidents of mistreatment of detainees and willful killing of civilians in Iraq, the Prosecutor began collecting information on these incidents and on related criminal proceedings that were undertaken by the States Parties whose nationals were allegedly responsible.[104]

The Prosecutor concluded that, in light of the available information, there was a reasonable basis to believe that crimes within the jurisdiction of the ICC had been committed. However, the Prosecutor did not believe that these crimes satisfied the gravity prong of Article 53's standard for initiating a formal investigation.[105] Assessing the gravity of the offenses in light of the number of victims resulting from each crime, the Prosecutor found that there were at most 12 victims of willful killing and a "limited" number of victims of inhuman treatment within the jurisdiction of the Court.[106] Noting that the Office of the Prosecutor was investigating three other situations that each involved thousands of willful killings as well as intentional and large-scale sexual violence and abductions, the Prosecutor concluded that the incidents in Iraq reviewed by the Office did not meet the required threshold of the Rome Statute.[107]

Because the situation did not meet the gravity threshold, the Prosecutor wrote that it was "unnecessary" to assess whether the situation satisfied Article 53's other two prongs, including Article 17's complementarity requirements.[108]

Selected Situations Undergoing Preliminary Analysis by the Prosecutor

Afghanistan

Preliminary Analysis in Afghanistan

On September 9, 2009, Prosecutor Moreno-Ocampo confirmed that his office was gathering information about possible war crimes committed by NATO soldiers, U.S. soldiers, and both Taliban and al Qaeda insurgents in Afghanistan.[109] The Prosecutor has declined since to provide further details about the specific incidents or allegations that the ICC is considering.[110] The Prosecutor also has not made public any decision regarding whether he is inclined to seek the Pre-Trial Chamber's permission to initiate a formal investigation.[111]

The United States has not officially supported or opposed the Chief Prosecutor's statements or information-gathering efforts regarding Afghanistan. Under questioning from Members of Congress in December

2009, Karl Eikenberry, U.S. Ambassador to Afghanistan, and General Stanley McChrystal, Commander of U.S. Forces Afghanistan and the International Security Assistance Force (ISAF), did not specifically refute the ICC's authority to investigate alleged crimes committed by U.S. and other NATO troops in Afghanistan. Instead, they stated that the U.S.-Afghanistan BIA and SOFA precluded the ICC from obtaining custody of members of the U.S. armed forces. In addition, alluding to the ICC's Article 17 on complementarity, they explained that any alleged wrongdoing would be properly investigated and prosecuted, if necessary, under the U.S. military justice system. General McChrystal and Ambassador Eikenberry stated that they were opposed to any ICC arrest and prosecution of members of the U.S. armed forces for actions taken in Afghanistan.[112]

ICC Jurisdiction over Alleged Crimes in Afghanistan

Unlike the Iraq situation discussed previously, the ICC has jurisdiction over alleged crimes that occurred in Afghanistan, even in cases where those offenses were committed by nationals of States that are not themselves States Parties to the ICC, because Afghanistan acceded to the Rome Statute on February 10, 2003. Afghanistan could choose to lodge a declaration with the Court accepting the Court's ad hoc jurisdiction over a period of time prior to that date under Article 12(3), thus empowering the Prosecutor to investigate crimes committed on Afghan soil after the Rome Statute entered force (July 1, 2002), but prior to Afghanistan's May 2003 ratification of it.

However, as with other cases, the ICC must consider not only whether it has jurisdiction over a situation, but also whether the situation meets the requirements described in Article 53 for a formal investigation and whether it is admissible under the complementarity requirements under Article 17. As a result, if the United States, for example, shows that it is willing and able to conduct "genuine" investigations and, where appropriate, prosecutions of nationals allegedly involved in criminal activities, those cases would become permanently inadmissible in the ICC. In addition, both countries can always seek to have the U.N. Security Council adopt a resolution pursuant to Article 16 of the Rome Statute to defer an investigation or prosecution for one year, with the option of renewal.[113]

Extradition of U.S. Nationals

Should the Prosecutor decide to proceed with a formal investigation and prosecution of crimes allegedly committed by U.S. citizens, a predictable concern is whether a foreign government could extradite U.S. suspects to the

ICC. As always, a country's ratification of the Rome Statute is not a prerequisite for the ICC's transmission of a request for the arrest and surrender of a suspect, but only those countries that are States Parties to the Rome Statute are mandated to comply with such a request. 114

Unlike the United States, Afghanistan is a party to the Rome Statute, having ratified it on February 10, 2003. In theory this means that Afghanistan is mandated to comply with a request from the ICC to surrender an American national. However, the United States and Afghanistan have also entered two agreements, the U.S-Afghanistan Bilateral Immunity Agreement (BIA)[115] and the U.S.-Afghanistan SOFA,[116] which present the kind of international obligations that, under Article 98, may preclude the ICC from requesting that Afghanistan surrender an American.[117] These Article 98 Agreements do not bar the ICC from asking States Parties *other than* Afghanistan to extradite the accused if the accused voluntarily enters their territory.[118] However, the effect that these two agreements would have on a similar request to *Afghanistan* is unclear given the debate over the meaning and applicability of Article 98. Without guidance from the ICC itself, it is impossible to know whether the Court would find that the BIA or the SOFA precludes an ICC request that Afghanistan surrender a U.S. national. It is also not clear whether Afghanistan would honor an extradition request from the ICC in light of any conflicting obligation imposed by the BIA or SOFA.

As discussed, there are at least two potential approaches that the ICC might take on this question in addition to the textualist reading of Article 98 on which the United States has relied in entering bilateral immunity agreements.[119] If the ICC agrees with the view that Article 98 preserves only SOFA-like obligations contained in international agreements, the Court would most likely interpret the U.S.-Afghanistan SOFA as preempting an ICC request that Afghanistan surrender U.S. *personnel*, but conclude that the U.S.-Afghanistan BIA does not preempt an ICC request that Afghanistan surrender any U.S. *citizens* present in Afghanistan who were not serving as U.S. personnel.[120] If, on the other hand, the ICC interprets Article 98 pursuant to either of the other two approaches discussed, namely (1) that Article 98 was intended to preempt requests to surrender that conflict with international obligations *predating* the sending State's entry into the ICC,[121] or (2) that Article 98 should be interpreted literally,[122] then a request to Afghanistan for the surrender of a U.S. citizen would most likely be deemed preempted by the BIA. While the ICC is the sole arbiter of the meaning and applicability of Article 98, political realities could weigh in favor of the U.S. position on the application of Article 98 to its BIA with Afghanistan.[123]

Gaza Strip

On January 22, 2009, the Palestinian National Authority (PNA) lodged a declaration pursuant to Article 12(3) of the Rome Statute with the Registrar of the ICC, accepting ICC ad hoc jurisdiction over alleged crimes committed during the December 2008/January 2009 conflict between Israeli and Hamas forces in the Gaza strip.[124] The ICC's jurisdiction over any alleged crimes would come solely from the PNA's declaration as neither Israel nor the PNA are States Parties to the Rome Statute.[125] However, the PNA's declaration is complicated by the fact that it has not been recognized as a State, and, absent this recognition, the PNA cannot confer on the Court ad hoc jurisdiction over offenses on its territory under Article 12.[126] This has raised concerns that the contentious issue of Palestinian statehood could come before the ICC.[127]

When the PNA lodged its declaration seeking to confer on the ICC ad hoc jurisdiction, the Office of the Prosecutor had received 213 communications from individuals and NGOs relating to the situation between Israel and the Palestinian Territories.[128] By February 13, 2009, less than a month later, that number had jumped to 326.[129] The Prosecutor has not released any further information about the status of its preliminary analysis into the Gaza Conflict.[130]

In September 2009, the U.N. Human Rights Council-established U.N. Commission of Inquiry on Gaza presented the Report of the U.N. Fact Finding Mission on the Gaza Conflict ("Goldstone Report"),[131] which found both war crimes and crimes against humanity had been committed in the Gaza conflict.[132] The report recommended that the U.N. Security Council (1) require Israel and the PNA to carry out national level investigations and prosecutions against those responsible for the crimes, and (2) if Israel and the PNA failed to conduct these proceedings within a six-month period, refer the situation to the ICC Prosecutor.[133] If the U.N. Security Council ultimately refers the situation to the ICC, then, under Article 13(b), the ICC Prosecutor will have jurisdiction even though neither Israel nor Palestine is a member of the ICC and the ICC may not deem Palestine a "state" under the Rome Statute.[134] The Security Council has referred only one situation to the ICC Prosecutor previously, and that referral resulted in the ICC Prosecutor opening a formal investigation into alleged war crimes in Darfur.[135]

The United States has generally opposed ICC involvement in investigating alleged crimes committed during the December 2008-January 2009 conflict between Israel and Hamas in the Gaza Strip. U.S. representatives in the United Nations have disagreed with the conclusions of the Goldstone Report, including the recommendation of a U.N. Security Council resolution to authorize an ICC investigation of alleged crimes. The United States was one of six members to vote against a resolution adopted by the U.N. Human Rights Council endorsing the findings of the Goldstone Report.[136] State Department spokesman Ian Kelly, in addition to disagreeing with the report's assessment of the actions taken by both sides to the conflict, also expressed the department's concern over calls in the report for the issue "to be taken up in international fora outside the Human Rights Council and in national courts of countries not party to the conflict."[137] Other statements by U.S. representatives have indicated the Obama Administration's preference that the Gaza issue be dealt with in the Human Rights Council and not in the ICC or the Security Council, where a vote on a resolution referring the alleged crimes to the ICC for investigation might occur.[138]

DEVELOPMENTS IN U.S. ICC POLICY

A shift in the overall U.S. government policy and treatment of the ICC is apparent from legislative and executive branch actions in recent years. As discussed earlier, the United States has based its opposition to the ICC on sovereignty concerns, the possibility for overreach by the ICC prosecutor, and the desire to protect members of the U.S. armed forces from politically motivated prosecutions before the Court. While these concerns do not seem to have abated, the views of the U.S. government, beginning under the George W. Bush Administration and continuing under the Obama Administration, appear to have shifted toward the conclusion that the ICC may sometimes serve as a useful tool in bringing perpetrators of the worst atrocities to justice. In addition, representatives of the Obama Administration have stated that despite continuing concerns about the Court, the United States can best protect and promote its interests through engaging with the ICC. Congress, after passing a number of pieces of legislation evincing opposition to the ICC and any effect of the Court on U.S. individuals or interests, has recently moved to roll back restrictions on U.S. foreign assistance to ICC States Parties.

Executive Branch Policy

Although remaining opposed to United States becoming a State Party to the Rome Statute, the Bush Administration in its second term took actions that evidenced an acceptance of the work and importance of the ICC in bringing perpetrators of atrocities to justice. In its first year, the Obama Administration was at times supportive of the ICC in its statements, and began to engage with the ICC, but did not adopt a policy to join the Court. The Obama Administration has undertaken an interagency review of its ICC policy and is expected to complete the review and make public its conclusions sometime in 2010.

United States Engagement with the ICC

In November 2009, the United States participated as an observer in the ICC's annual Assembly of States Parties in The Hague. In announcing the decision, Stephen Rapp, the U.S. Ambassador-atLarge for War Crimes Issues, stated, "Our government has now made the decision that Americans will return to engagement with the ICC."[139] He insisted, however, that the United States still does not intend to become party to the Rome Statute at this time.[140] Ambassador Rapp specifically mentioned continuing concerns over the possibility that U.S. service members "might be subject to politically inspired prosecutions."[141]

Both Ambassador Rapp and the State Department Legal Advisor, Harold Koh, attended the ICC Assembly of States Parties. In his remarks to the Assembly, Ambassador Rapp asserted that while not a State Party to the Rome Statute, the United States did not at any point abandon its commitment to bringing perpetrators of atrocities to justice, including through international criminal tribunals such as those created by the United Nations for crimes committed in the former Yugoslavia and Rwanda.[142] He stated that there are instances when only the international community, working together, can ensure justice is done, and cited the U.S. support of and cooperation in the ICC's investigation into alleged crimes in Darfur.[143] He also explained the U.S. intention to gain a "better understanding of the issues being considered [by the ICC States Parties] and the workings of the Court."[144] Ambassador Rosemary DiCarlo, U.S. Alternate Representative to the United Nations for Special Political Affairs, stated in the Security Council on December 4, 2009, "Although the United States is not a party to the Rome Statute, the United States was pleased to participate last week for the first time as an observer to the Assembly of States Parties to the Rome Statute. This decision reflected the U.S. commitment to engage with the international community on issues that affect our foreign policy interests."[145]

Ambassador Rapp has also stated that the United States will participate in the Review Conference of the Rome Statute, to take place in Kampala, Uganda, in May-June 2010.[146] At the Assembly, he spoke about the possibility of amending the Rome Statute to include the crime of aggression within the ICC's jurisdiction, an issue that will be a topic of discussion at the 2010 Review Conference. His remarks reflected the continuing U.S. opposition to inclusion of such a crime within the Court's purview, stating that determining and dealing with aggression is the responsibility of the U.N. Security Council, and that decisions on ICC prosecution of aggression could draw the ICC "into a political thicket that could threaten its perceived impartiality."[147]

U.S. Actions in the United Nations Concerning the ICC

On March 31, 2005, the U.N. Security Council by a vote of 11 in favor with four Members abstaining, including the United States, adopted Resolution 1593, which referred allegations of crimes committed by President Omar Hassan Ahmad al-Bashir of Sudan to the ICC prosecutor. On July 31, 2008, the United States abstained in a Council vote on Resolution 1828, which contained language implying that the Security Council would consider an Article 16 deferral of the Bashir prosecution under the Rome Statute.[148] The Obama Administration has opposed an Article 16 deferral of the prosecution of President Bashir.[149] Upon the issuance of the arrest warrant for President Bashir, Ambassador Susan Rice, U.S. Permanent Representative to the United Nations, released a statement calling for restraint from all parties in Darfur, and cooperation from the government of Sudan.[150] With regard to the enforcement of the warrant for the arrest of the President of Sudan, Ambassador Rapp stated in his confirmation hearing that it is the Obama Administration's intent to support ICC efforts to enforce the arrest warrant.[151]

The Obama Administration has also reversed a Bush Administration policy to oppose language in Security Council resolutions referring to the ICC.[152] On September 30, 2009, the U.N. Security Council, chaired by U.S. Secretary of State Hillary Clinton, unanimously adopted Resolution 1888, which contains a specific reference to sexual violence crimes listed in the Rome Statute.[153]

Obama Administration Statements Concerning the ICC

Although the Obama Administration has expressed general support for the ICC and has stated that the ICC may sometimes service as a useful tool for prosecuting war crimes and other atrocities, the Administration has not announced a policy to automatically back every proposed ICC investigation and prosecution. Instead, as Ambassador Rapp stated before the ICC Assembly of States Parties, the United States will support international tribunals when they are necessary to achieve justice, but will continue to place "greatest importance" on helping individual States set up their own systems of justice to deal with the worst atrocities.[154] The Obama Administration has treated possible U.S. adherence to the ICC Statute as a separate issue from its willingness to support the Court's work, continuing to cite the security of U.S. armed forces as a stumbling block to the U.S. joining as a State Party to the Rome Statute.

ICC's Effectiveness and the United States as a Possible State Party

Indications that the Obama Administration would shift U.S. policy toward the ICC were apparent early on, with Administration representatives characterizing the ICC as a body with potential to provide justice for victims of atrocities. In response to written questions from Senator John Kerry prior to her nomination hearing to become Secretary of State, Hillary Clinton stated that the Obama Administration would end U.S. "hostility" to the ICC, and would support the work of the ICC.[155] She stated that the ICC had so far operated with "professionalism and fairness," citing the ICC's work on cases in Darfur, Congo, and Uganda.[156] She explained that the Obama Administration would conduct a full review of the U.S. position on becoming a State Party to the Rome Statute, citing the continuing concern about the security of members of the U.S. armed forces deployed overseas. In January 2009, U.N. Ambassador Susan Rice stated that the ICC is "look[ing] to become an important and credible instrument for trying to hold accountable the senior leadership responsible for atrocities committed in the Congo, Uganda and Darfur."[157]

In August 2009, Secretary of State Hillary Clinton spoke about the fact that the United States had not become party to the Rome Statute. Responding to arguments regarding an apparent contradiction between U.S. support for a possible ICC investigation into the massacres that marked the 2007 elections in Kenya and the U.S. refusal to become party to the Rome Statute, she stated it is "a great regret" that the United States is not a party to the Rome Statute, adding, "I think we could have worked out some of the challenges that are raised concerning our membership by our own government, but that has not yet come to pass."[158] She asserted, however, that the United States will support the ICC in its investigations and prosecutions.

Continuing U.S. Preference for National Justice Systems and Special Tribunals

The Obama Administration has continued to adhere to a policy of encouraging local and national justice systems to take up prosecutions of alleged atrocities, or to create special tribunals within communities where the violence has occurred. Ambassador Rapp, during his nomination hearing, stated that the Office for War Crimes Issues is committed to bringing individuals to account for war crimes and other atrocities. He expressed the U.S. government's continuing preference for local and specialized forms of justice for such crimes, but acknowledged the need for international efforts in some cases:

> Our first preference should be for a process of accountability at the level that is closest to the affected communities. However, peace and reconciliation can best be assured by a justice system that is independent and has sufficient capacity to hold to account those bearing the greatest responsibility for atrocities. Achieving accountability in different situations will require varying levels of assistance and international participation.[159]

This statement seems to reflect the continuation of the view that the United States will cooperate with the ICC when it believes it is a useful forum for bringing criminals to justice, but that it will encourage other special courts or the use of national justice systems when feasible.[160] This position is, arguably, consistent with the principle of complementarity that underlies the ICC because it sees ICC involvement as limited to those situations when local justice systems lack the capacity to effectively deal with alleged atrocities.

This approach has been reinforced in Obama Administration comments concerning specific ICC investigations and other proceedings. With regard to the 2007 election violence in Kenya, Secretary Clinton in August 2009 stated that it is the hope of the United States that Kenya can use its own national justice system to bring alleged criminals to justice, therefore negating the need for the ICC to conduct prosecutions.[161] The United States has urged Kenya to create a special tribunal to prosecute alleged perpetrators of the violence, but has also urged Kenyan officials to cooperate fully with the ICC in its investigations into these criminal allegations.[162] If Kenya cannot set up a special tribunal, U.S. diplomatic officials have stated support for action by the ICC.[163]

In the Democratic Republic of the Congo (DRC), the ICC has brought charges against certain military commanders for war crimes, crimes against humanity, and sexual crimes. The United States has not opposed these cases, but has stated that other mechanisms of justice and accountability are needed in the DRC.[164]

ICC's Effect on Peace Settlements

Some observers have criticized the ICC for effectively discouraging the settlement of armed conflicts, arguing that alleged perpetrators of war crimes and other atrocities will lose any incentive to bring hostilities to an end if an ICC warrant for their arrest is issued. In addition, some have criticized the United States and others for negotiating with governments whose representatives are currently wanted by the ICC for alleged crimes. Ambassador Rapp has addressed these concerns, claiming that while the United States is currently working to achieve a peace settlement with the Sudanese government and rebel groups in Darfur, for example, such efforts are not "inconsistent with pressing for accountability for those responsible for serious violations of international humanitarian law."[165] In addition, he stated that the indictments of Charles Taylor by the Special Court for Sierra Leone and of Joseph Kony by the ICC enhanced, rather than hindered, prospects for peace in Sierra Leone and Uganda, respectively.[166]

Bilateral Immunity Agreements

As explained previously, the United States has executed BIAs with scores of countries, in the hope of limiting the ICC's ability to request that States Parties surrender U.S. nationals to the ICC. The United States concluded the most recent BIA in 2007, with Montenegro. CRS has located the texts of 96 BIAs, but there are six additional BIAs that were reported but not located. A number of countries have concluded BIAs with the United States despite not being States Parties to the Rome Statute. These agreements remain in effect, although, as discussed above, their effectiveness under international law has been questioned.

Recent Congressional Action

Although several provisions in legislation opposing U.S. adherence to and support for the ICC Statute remain in effect, recent Congresses have eliminated or refrained from renewing sanctions provisions that affect U.S. assistance for countries that are ICC States Parties. Although these actions could be interpreted as indicating a change in Congress's position towards the

ICC, the changes might also be interpreted as being primarily rooted in a concern that sanctions may have begun to hurt U.S. interests.

Section 2007 of the American Servicemembers' Protection Act

Enacted in 2002, Section 2007[167] of the American Servicemembers' Protection Act (ASPA) prohibited U.S. military assistance to ICC States Parties. Such assistance was defined in Section 2013(13) of the act as assistance provided under chapter 2 (Military Assistance) or 5 (International Military Education and Training, or IMET) of part II of the Foreign Assistance Act of 1961, as amended (FAA, P.L. 87-195), as well as credit sales of defense articles or services under Section 23 of the Arms Export Control Act, as amended (AECA, P.L. 90-629; 22 U.S.C. § 2463).

Section 2007 contained a general prohibition on assistance, two bases for presidential waivers of that prohibition, and an exemption from the prohibition. Subsection (a) stated that effective one year after the date on which the Rome Statute enters into force, no U.S. military assistance may be provided to States Parties to the ICC. Subsection (b) provided that the President could waive, without prior notice to Congress, the prohibition with regard to a country if he determines and reports to Congress that it is in the U.S. national interest to do so. Subsection (c) authorized the President to waive, again without prior notice to Congress, the prohibition with regard to a country if (1) the country entered into a BIA with the United States and (2) the President reported the agreement to Congress. Subsection (d) exempted NATO members, designated major non-NATO allies (MNNAs),[168] and Taiwan from the prohibition.

Nethercutt Amendment Provisions

Provisions enacted in the 2005, 2006, and 2008 Foreign Operations Appropriations bills (so-called "Nethercutt Amendment" provisions[169]) contained similar funding prohibitions for Economic Support Fund (ESF) assistance to ICC States Parties:

- Section 574 of the Foreign Operations, Export Financing, and Related Programs Appropriations Act, 2005 (FY2005 Appropriations Act; Division D of P.L. 108- 447; 118 Stat. 3027) prohibited Economic Support Fund (ESF) assistance to ICC States Parties for funds available through September 30, 2006.

- Section 574 of the Foreign Operations, Export Financing, and Related Programs Appropriations Act, 2006 (FY2006 Appropriations Act; P.L. 109-102; 119 Stat. 2229) contained the same general ESF prohibition for funds available through September 30, 2007.[170]
- Section 671 of the Department of State, Foreign Operations, and Related Programs Appropriations Act, 2008 (FY2008 Appropriations Act; Division J of P.L. 110-161; 121 Stat. 2354) prohibited ESF assistance for ICC States Parties with regard to funds available through September 30, 2009.

Each Nethercutt Amendment provision differed somewhat from the other two. Section 574 of the FY2005 Appropriations Act contained a general prohibition on ESF assistance, two bases for a Presidential waiver of the prohibition, and an exemption from the prohibition. Subsection (a) prohibited the use of ESF funds to assist a country that is a party to the ICC and that has not entered into an Article 98 agreement with the United States. Subsection (b) authorized the President to waive, without prior notice to Congress, this prohibition for NATO members, MNNAs, or Taiwan, if he determines and reports to Congress that it is important to U.S. *national security interests* to do so (emphasis not in legislation).[171] Subsection (c) allows the President to waive, without prior notice to Congress, the prohibition with regard to a country if the country entered into an agreement with the United States pursuant to Article 98 of the Rome Statute preventing the ICC from proceeding against U.S. personnel in such country, and if the President reports to Congress on the agreement. Subsection (d) provided that the prohibition does not apply to countries otherwise eligible for assistance under the Millennium Challenge Act of 2003 (MCA, Title VI of Division D of the Consolidated Appropriations Act, 2004; P.L. 108-199).

Section 574 of the FY2006 Appropriations Act contained the general prohibition on ESF assistance, two bases for a Presidential waiver of the prohibition, an exemption from the prohibition in that section, and an additional exemption from the prohibition contained in the Nethercutt Amendment provision from the 2005 Act. Subsection (a) provided the identical prohibition on ESF funds to ICC States Parties without an Article 98 agreement with the United States. Subsection (b) also provided for a Presidential determination justifying a waiver of the prohibition, but it required prior notice to Congress, included "such other country as he may determine" along with NATO members, MNNAs, and Taiwan as eligible to receive the waiver, and changed the standard from a determination of national *security* interest to one of national interest. Subsection (c) of the FY2006 Act provision is similar to that of FY2005, allowing the President to waive if a country entered an Article 98 agreement, except this waiver also became dependent on prior notice to Congress. Subsection (d) contained the identical exemption from the prohibition for MCA-eligible countries. Subsection (e) exempted democracy and rule of law programs and activities from the FY2005 Nethercutt Amendment's prohibition on ESF funds to ICC States Parties.

Subsections (a) through (d) of Section 671 of the FY2008 Appropriations Act were identical to those of Section 574 of the FY2006 Appropriations Act, with the same general prohibition; national interest waiver eligibility for NATO, MNNAs, Taiwan, and "such other" countries as the President may determine; Article 98 agreement waiver; and MCA-eligible country exemption. There was no further subsection concerning previous Nethercutt Amendment provisions.

Modifications to the ASPA/Nethercutt Sanctions Policy

Although Section 2007 of ASPA and the Nethercutt Amendment provisions articulated a strong policy of opposition to the ICC, in line with the U.S. policy toward the Court during much of the Bush Administration, questions from within the executive branch on the costs and benefits of such sanctions surfaced as early as 2006. Secretary of State Condoleezza Rice was quoted as describing the sanctions as akin to "shooting ourselves in the foot" when they prohibited military aid to key U.S. allies. The 2005 Quadrennial Defense Review characterized APSA's restrictions as a burden on the U.S. military in its efforts to combat terrorism. In addition, President Bush granted nearly 90 waivers of ASPA or Nethercutt prohibitions during his Administration on national interest grounds where no BIA was in place, revealing a substantial need to continue military and ESF assistance to U.S. partners that were also ICC States Parties. A number of Members of Congress shared the concerns of certain Bush Administration officials.

In 2006, Congress amended Section 2013(13)(A) of the ASPA to remove IMET funding from the definition of U.S. military assistance (Section 1222 of Division A of the John Warner National Defense Authorization Act for Fiscal Year 2007, P.L. 109-364). In 2007, Section 1212(a) of the National Defense Authorization Act for Fiscal Year 2008 (P.L. 110-181; 122 Stat. 371) repealed Section 2007 of ASPA altogether, thus ending the prohibition on FAA military assistance and AECA military credit sales for States Parties to the ICC. After being included in the previous three bills, Nethercutt Amendment language was not included in the most recent foreign operations appropriations legislation (Department of State, Foreign Operations, and Related Programs Appropriations Act, 2009; Division H of P.L. 111-8). At present, therefore, ICC-related prohibitions on military and ESF assistance are no longer operative.

Legislation Proposed in the 111th Congress

To date, no bills have been introduced in the current Congress relating to the ICC or U.S. becoming party to the Rome Statute, or participating in or cooperating with the Court. Members in the House have proposed non-binding resolutions concerning the ICC as it relates to alleged atrocities.

H.Res. 867: This resolution characterizes the Goldstone Report concerning the 2008-2009 conflict in Gaza as biased and unbalanced in its criticism of Israel's actions during that conflict. It calls on President Obama to veto "any United Nations Security Council resolution that endorses the contents of this report, seeks to act upon the recommendations contained in this report, or calls on any other international body to take further action regarding this report." The Goldstone Report recommended that the Security Council refer the Gaza case to the ICC prosecutor to investigate allegations of war crimes if no prosecutions by national justice systems are undertaken within 6 months. It passed the House on November 3, 2009.

H.Res. 241: This resolution commends the ICC for issuing a warrant for the arrest of Omar Hassan Ahmad al-Bashir, President of the Republic of the Sudan. It was referred to the House Foreign Affairs Committee on March 12, 2009.

H.Con.Res. 97: This concurrent resolution calls on the President to (1) support U.N. Security Council referrals of atrocities to the ICC; (2) state as U.S. policy a commitment to support the Rome Statute and to reactivate the United States as signatory to the Statute; (3) cooperate with ICC investigations unless it is not in the U.S. national interest; (4) participate as observer at the annual ICC Assembly of States Parties; (5) and grant waivers, based on national interest, of prohibitions against assistance and cooperation with the ICC. It was referred to the House Foreign Affairs Committee on April 2, 2009.

End Notes

[1] *See* Rome Statute of the International Criminal Court, Preamble, U.N. Doc. A/CONF.183/9 (1998) (hereinafter "Rome Statute"). These include genocide, crimes against humanity, war

crimes, and potentially the crime of aggression, if the Assembly of States Parties is able to reach an agreement defining it. *Id.* Art. 5(1).

[2] Rome Statute, Art. 24(1). Because there is no retroactivity, a crime committed before that date can not be tried before the ICC. *Id.*

[3] *See* International Criminal Court, Situations and Cases, http://www.icc-cpi.int /Menus /ICC/ Situations+and+Cases (last visited Dec. 8, 2009). These referrals involved allegations of war crimes in three countries: the Republic of Uganda, the Democratic Republic of Congo, and the Central African Republic. Each referral was submitted by the country seeking investigation into possible war crimes committed within its territory.

[4] SC Res. 1593, U.N. Doc. S/RES/1593 (2005).

[5] Alina Ioana Apreotesei, *International Court at Work: First Cases and Situations*, 5 EYES ON THE ICC 1, 1 (2008).

[6] Press Conference by the Prosecutor of the International Criminal Court, International Criminal Court (Nov. 26, 2009), http://www.icc-cpi.int/Menus/ICC/Press+and+Media/Press+ Releases (follow "Press conference by ICC Prosecutor Luis Moreno-Ocampo related to the situation in Kenya") (last visited Dec. 8, 2009).

[7] Judge Phillippe Kirsch, President of the ICC, Address at the Rayburn House Office Building (Feb. 13, 2009), http://globalsolutions.org/files/general/Philippe_Kirsch_2-13-09.pdf; American Non-Governmental Organizations Coalition for the International Criminal Court (AMICC),Work of the Prosecutor, ICC Activities, http://www.amicc.org /icc_ activities. html#pstatements (last visited Dec. 8, 2009). One of the suspects accused of committing international crimes in Uganda, Raska Lukwiya, died before he was taken into custody. International Criminal Court, Situations and Cases, http://www.icc-cpi.int /Menus /ICC/ Situations+and+Cases (last visited Dec. 8, 2009). The case against him has since been terminated. International Criminal Court, Uganda, http://www.icc-cpi.int/Menus/ICC/ Situations+and+Cases/Situations/Situation+ICC+0204 (last visited Dec. 8, 2009).

[8] Situations and Cases, International Criminal Court *available at* http://www.icc-cpi.int/Menus /ICC/Situations+and+Cases (last visited Dec. 8, 2009).

[9] Rome Statute, Art. 77. Typically imprisonment must be for no longer than thirty years unless a term of life imprisonment is justified by the extreme gravity of the crime and the circumstances of the convicted person. *Id.*

[10] *See* Ruth Wedgwood et. al., *The United States and the Statute of Rome,* 95 AM. J. INT'L L. 124 (2001) (commenting that the United States has "repeatedly and publicly declared its support in principle" for an international criminal court). Congress expressed its support for the ICC on the condition that its operation would not infringe upon the rights of U.S. citizens. *See, e.g.,* Foreign Operations Appropriations Act § 599E, P.L. 101-513, 104 Stat. 2066-2067 (1990) (expressing the sense of the Congress that "the United States should explore the need for the establishment of an International Criminal Court" and that "the establishment of such a court or courts for the more effective prosecution of international criminals should not derogate from established standards of due process, the rights of the accused to a fair trial and the sovereignty of individual nations").

[11] *See* U.N. International Criminal Court: Hearings before the Subcomm. on International Operations of the Senate Foreign Relations Committee, 105th Cong. (1998) (testimony of David J. Scheffer, Ambassador-at-Large for War Crimes Issues).

[12] *See* Wedgwood, *supra* note 10, at 124 (noting that the final vote for the Statute was 120 in favor to 7 against). For a detailed history of the ICC and the negotiations of the Rome Statute, read CRS Report RL31437, *International Criminal Court: Overview and Selected Legal Issues*, by Jennifer K. Elsea.

[13] *See* Statement on the Rome Treaty on the International Criminal Court, 37 Weekly Comp. Pres Doc 4 (December 31, 2000).

[14] Press Statement, International Criminal Court: Letter to U.N. Secretary General Kofi Annan (May 26, 2002); International Criminal Law, 2002 DIGEST OF UNITED STATES PRACTICE IN INTERNATIONAL LAW, at 148.

[15] *See* Marc Grossman, Under Secretary for Political Affairs, Remarks to the Center for Strategic and International Studies, Washington, D.C., (May 6, 2002), prepared remarks available at http://www.mtholyoke.edu/acad/intrel/bush/rome.htm (last visited Dec. 31, 2009).

[16] Bryan MacPherson, *Authority of the Security Council to Exempt Peacekeepers from International Criminal Court Proceedings*, ASIL INSIGHTS (July 2002), *available at* http://www.asil.org/insigh89.cfm. *See* Colum Lynch, *Dispute Threatens U.N. Role in Bosnia; U.S. Wields Veto in Clash over War Crimes Court*, WASH. POST, July 1, 2002, at A1.

[17] SC Res. 1422, U.N. Doc. S/RES/1422 (2002). The resolution read, in part, "[C]onsistent with the provisions of Article 16 of the Rome Statute, [] the ICC, if a case arises involving current or former officials or personnel from a contributing State not a Party to the Rome Statute over acts or omissions relating to a United Nations established or authorized operation, shall for a twelve-month period starting 1 July 2002 not commence or proceed with investigation or prosecution of any such case, unless the Security Council decides otherwise."

[18] Article 16 reads: "No investigation or prosecution may be commenced or proceeded with under this Statute for a period of 12 months after the Security Council, in a resolution adopted under Chapter VII of the Charter of the United Nations, has requested the Court to that effect; that request may be renewed by the Council under the same conditions."

[19] SC Res. 1487, U.N. Doc. S/RES/1487 (2003).

[20] *E.g.* Agreement Regarding the Surrender of Persons to the International Criminal Court, U.S.-Israel, Aug. 4, 2002, Temp. State Dep't No. 04-16, KAV 6368; Agreement Regarding the Surrender of Persons to the International Criminal Court, U.S.-Pak., July 21, 2003, Temp. State. Dep't No. 04-03, KAV 6356. Of particular interest given recent events is the reciprocal Bilateral Immunity Agreement between the Transitional Islamic State of Afghanistan and the United States. Agreement Regarding the Surrender of Persons to the International Criminal Court, U.S.-Afghanistan, Aug. 23, 2003, Temp. State Dep't No. 03-119, KAV 6308. To read the text of many Article 98 Agreements, visit the Georgetown Law Library's Article 98 Agreements Research Guide at http://www.ll. georgetown. edu/ guides/article_98.cfm (last visited Dec. 19, 2009).

[21] *See* Rome Statute, Art. 98(2); Ambassador Pierre-Richard Prosper, Remarks on the Foreign Affairs Consequences of America's Absence (March 7, 2003) *in* 8 UCLA J. INT'L L. & FOR. AFF. 17, at 20. There are two opposite perspectives on Article 98 agreements. The first is that these agreements are consistent with the spirit and text of the ICC because they merely ensure that the right of the United States not to be treated as a party to the Rome Statute is respected. *E.g. id.* at 20-21. The second is that these agreements are "at worst legally incompatible with, and at best a misuse of, article 98." *E.g.*, Max du Plessis, *South Africa's Response to American Hostility Towards the International Criminal Court*, 30 S. AFR. Y.B. INT'L L. 112, 123 (2005).

[22] See section VI(B), *infra.*

[23] Congress also enacted certain provisions restricting the use of funds to assist the ICC prior to the creation of the Court. Sections 705 and 706 of the Admiral James W. Nance and Meg Donovan Foreign Relations Authorization Act, Fiscal Years 2000 and 2001 (H.R. 3427

(106th Cong.), enacted by reference in Section 1000(a)(7) of P.L. 106-113; 22 U.S.C. §§ 7401, 7402) prohibit the use of appropriated funds to support the ICC unless the United States has joined the Court pursuant to a treaty as set out in the U.S. Constitution, and prohibit the use of such funds to extradite or transfer U.S. citizens to the ICC.

[24] For a detailed discussion of ASPA, see CRS Report RL31495, *U.S. Policy Regarding the International Criminal Court (ICC)*, by Jennifer K. Elsea.

[25] A detailed discussion of the Nethercutt Amendment provisions is provided in section VI(B), *infra*.

[26] See U.S. Actions in the United Nations Concerning the ICC, *infra*.

[27] See U.S. Engagement with the ICC, *infra*.

[28] Kirsch, *supra* note 7.

[29] *See* Rome Statute, Art. 12.

[30] Rome Statute, Arts. 12(2), 13(b); Kirsch, *supra* note 7.

[31] Rome Statute, Art. 12(3).

[32] *Id.*

[33] *Id.* at Art. 17. Notably, the ICC, like other judicial bodies, retains the power and duty to determine the boundaries of its jurisdiction. The Prosecutor v. Joseph Kony et. al., Case No. ICC-02/04-01/05, Decision on the Admissibility of the Case under Article 19(1) of the Statute, 45 (March 10, 2009) *available at* http://www.icc-cpi.int/ Menus/ ICC/ Situations +and+Cases/Situations [follow hyperlinks for "Situation in Uganda" then "Related Cases," "Court Records," and "Pre-Trial Chamber II"].

[34] *Id.*

[35] *See* Rome Statute, Art. 1.

[36] *See* Kirsch, *supra* note 7.

[37] The Prosecutor v. Germain Katanga and Mathieu Ngudjolo Chui, Case No. ICC-01/04-01/07, Reasons for the Oral Decision on the Motion Challenging the Admissibility of the Case (Article 19 of the Statute), ¶ 75 (June 16, 2009). The Katanga case is an example of the necessary interaction between Articles 17 and 19 of the Rome Statute. The two articles are meant to work in concert as Article 19(1) permits the Court to determine, *sua sponte*, whether Article 17 bars a particular case, and Article 19(2) sets guidelines for challenges raised under Article 17 by defendants or States.

[38] Rome Statute, Art. 17(2).

[39] *See* The Prosecutor v. Germain Katanga and Mathieu Ngudjolo Chui, Case No. ICC-01/04-01/07, Reasons for the Oral Decision on the Motion Challenging the Admissibility of the Case (Article 19 of the Statute), ¶ 90 (June 16, 2009).

[40] *Id.*

[41] Rome Statute, Art. 17(3).

[42] Rome Statute, Art. 42(4). The Assembly of States Parties is comprised of a representative of each State Party. *Id. at* Art. 112. Non-Party States who have signed the Rome Statute may participate in the Assembly as observers but may not vote. *Id.* The Assembly assists the administration of the ICC by, for example, adopting the budget. *Id.* In addition, the Assembly may amend the Rome Statute if two-thirds of the Assembly vote in favor of the amendment. *Id.* at Art. 121. The Assembly convenes at least once a year at either The Hague or at the Headquarters of the United Nations in New York City. *Id.* at Art. 112(6).

[43] Rome Statute, Art. 42(3).

[44] Rome Statute, Art. 42(4).

[45] Rome Statute, Art. 42(1).

[46] *Id.*

[47] Rome Statute, Art. 42(7).

[48] Rome Statute, Art. 89(1).

[49] *See id.* Parties to the Rome Statute, on the other hand, must also ensure that there are procedures available under their national law for this kind of cooperation. Rome Statute, Art. 89(1); Art. 88.

[50] Rome Statute, Art. 98. *See also* International Criminal Court Rules of Procedure and Evidence, Rule 195.2 (" The Court may not proceed with a request for the surrender of a person without the consent of a sending State if, under [A]rticle 98, paragraph 2, such a request would be inconsistent with obligations under an international agreement pursuant to which the consent of a sending State is required prior to the surrender of a person of that State to the Court.")

[51] 155 U.N.T.S. 331 (1969).

[52] Vienna Convention on the Law of Treaties, Art. 31.1. Although the United States is not a party to the Vienna Convention, it recognizes the VCLT as generally signifying customary international law. *See e.g.* Fujitsu Ltd. v. Fed'l Exp. Corp., 247 F.3d 423 (2d. Cir. 2001) (describing U.S. recognition of the Vienna Convention "as, in large part, the authoritative guide to current treaty law and practice.").

[53] Article 98(2) of the Rome Statute reads: "The Court may not proceed with a request for surrender which would require the requested State to act inconsistently with its obligations under international agreements pursuant to which the consent of a sending State is required to surrender a person of that State to the Court, unless the Court can first obtain the cooperation of the sending State ..." The first paragraph of Article 98 reads largely the same but refers to "obligations under international law" and "diplomatic immunity of a person or property" rather than to "international agreements."

[54] du Plessis, *South Africa's Response to American Hostility Towards the ICC*, 30 S. AFR. Y. B. INT'L L. 112, 117 (2005); Kimberly Prost & Claus Kreß, *Article 98: Cooperation with Respect to Waiver of Immunity and Consent to Surrender, in* COMMENTARY ON THE ROME STATUTE OF THE INTERNATIONAL CRIMINAL COURT: OBSERVERS' NOTES, ARTICLE BY ARTICLE 1615 (Otto Triffterer ed., Hart Publishing 2008) (1999) (writing that the negotiations on Article 98(2) were undertaken with a view towards preserving SOFAs, which confined the competence and jurisdiction of the sending country to acts perpetrated by that state's citizens in the performance of their official duty). *See* Mahnoush H. Arsanjani, *The Rome Statute of the International Criminal Court*, 93 AM. J. INT'L L. 22, 41 (1999) ("[T]he main concern in [Article 98] is to respect the obligations of host States under status-of-forces agreements. Under these agreements, the forces of a sending state may remain under its jurisdiction for some or all matters, and not under that of the host state.").

[55] For more on Status of Forces Agreements (SOFAs), read CRS Report RL34531, *Status of Forces Agreement (SOFA): What Is It, and How Has It Been Utilized?*, by R. Chuck Mason.

[56] Kimberly Prost & Claus Kreß, *supra* note 54, at 1616.

[57] Vienna Convention on the Law of Treaties, Art. 18 ("A State is obliged to refrain from acts which would defeat the object and purpose of a treaty when: (a) it has signed the treaty or has exchanged instruments constituting the treaty subject to ratification, acceptance or approval, until it shall have made its intention clear not to become a party to the treaty; or (b) it has expressed its consent to be bound by the treaty, pending the entry into force of the treaty and provided that such entry into force is not unduly delayed.").

[58] du Plessis, *supra* note 54, at 125 (2005). *E.g.* Rome Statute, Arts. 86, 87(7) (requiring parties to the Rome Statute to cooperate with the ICC).

[59] Prost & Kreß, *supra* note 54, at 1616.

[60] *Id.* at 1603. Arguably, however, these contemplations should not be equated with the intent of the Article 98(2) drafters because, if the U.S. delegation disclosed these contemplations to other participants in the negotiations, that disclosure probably did not happen until very late in the day. *Id.*

[61] *Id.* at 1616.

[62] *Id.*

[63] *Id.* at 1617.

[64] United Nations Diplomatic Conference of Plenipotentiaries on the Establishment of an International Criminal Court, Report of the Preparatory Committee on the Establishment of an International Criminal Court 134 (1998), *available at* http://www. un.org/ law/ n9810105.pdf. *See* Prost & Kreß, *supra* note 54, at 1617.

[65] Prost & Kreß, *supra* note 54, at 1616.

[66] *See id.* at 1603. *See also* Rome Statute, Arts. 4(1) (stating that the Court has "such legal capacity as may be necessary for the exercise of its functions and the fulfillment of its purpose"), 19(1) (providing that "the Court shall satisfy itself that it has jurisdiction in any case brought before it"); *Joseph Kony*, *supra* note 33, at 45 (referring to its previous discussions of the "well-known and fundamental principle that any judicial body, including any international tribunal, retains the power and the duty to determine the boundaries of its own jurisdiction and competence."). This suggests that whether the ICC has the authority to issue a particular request for surrender will be determined by the Court, which does not need to consider how the requested country interprets its potentially conflicting international obligations. *Id.*

[67] Prost & Kreß, *supra* note 54, at 1616.

[68] *See id.*

[69] *See id.* As Prost and Kreß describe the issue, "[A]ny determination by the Court that no conflicting international obligation exists will leave the requested State Party with the risk that the Court's determination of the international legal obligation is wrong."

[70] Rome Statute, Art. 53(1)(a).

[71] Rome Statute, Art. 53(1)(b); Art. 17. For a discussion of the requirements for complementarity, *see supra* notes 35-41 and accompanying text.

[72] Rome Statute, Art. 53(1)(c).

[73] Rome Statute, Art. 15(2).

[74] *Id.*

[75] OFFICE OF THE PROSECUTOR, INTERNATIONAL CRIMINAL COURT, RESPONSE TO COMMUNICATIONS RECEIVED CONCERNING IRAQ 9 (2006), *available at* http://www.icc-cpi.int/Menus/ICC/Structure+of+ the+Court/Office+ of+the+Prosecutor /Comm+and+Ref/Iraq/.

[76] *See id.* at 8. The Rome Statute provides a little clarification on the meaning of grave in Article 8(1)'s definition of war crimes, indicating that those that are committed "as part of a plan or policy or as part of a large-scale commission of such crimes" are perhaps more grave for Article 17's purposes than those that did not occur on a large-scale or as part of a plan or policy. *See* Rome Statute, Art. 8(1).

[77] *See* OFFICE OF THE PROSECUTOR, *supra* note 75, at 8-9. The Prosecutor has also hinted that some crimes, such as "willful killing or rape," are more serious than others, but has not elucidated a clear standard in that area. *Id.* at 9.

[78] *Id.* at 1; OFFICE OF THE PROSECUTOR, INTERNATIONAL CRIMINAL COURT, VISIT OF THE MINISTER OF JUSTICE OF THE PALESTINIAN NATIONAL AUTHORITY, MR. ALI KHASHAN, TO THE ICC (Feb. 6, 2009), http://www.icc-cpi.int/Menus/ICC/Structure+of+the+Court/Office+of+the+Prosecutor/Comm+and+Ref/Palestine (follow "Visit of the Minister of Justice of the Palestinian National Authority"). Between July of 2002 and February 2006, the Office of the Prosecutor received 1,732 communications on situations in 139 countries, but only 10 of those situations were subject to an intensive preliminary examination, and even fewer resulted in a request for authority to investigate. OFFICE OF THE PROSECUTOR, *supra* note 75, at 1.

[79] Rome Statute, Art. 15(3).

[80] *Id.* at Art. 15(4).

[81] *Id.* at Art. 15(6).

[82] OFFICE OF THE PROSECUTOR, *supra* note 78; Press Release, Office of the Prosecutor, International Criminal Court (Oct. 14, 2009 http://www.icc-cpi.int/Menus/ICC/Structure+of+the+Court/Office+ of+the+Prosecutor (follow "Communications and Referrals" hyperlink and then "ICC Prosecutor confirms situation in Guinea under examination").

[83] *See* OFFICE OF THE PROSECUTOR, *supra* note 75, 4.

[84] *Id. See also* International Criminal Court's Rules of Procedure and Evidence, Rules 46, 49(1).

[85] OFFICE OF THE PROSECUTOR, *supra* note 75, at 4. Pursuant to this policy, the Office of the Prosecutor has released, and made available on its website, the reasons behind the Prosecutor's decisions not to initiate investigations on situations in Iraq and Venezuela. *See id.*

[86] *See generally id.*

[87] *Id.* at 3.

[88] *Id.*

[89] OFFICE OF THE PROSECUTOR, *supra* note 75, at 3.

[90] *Id.*

[91] *Id.* at 2.

[92] *Id.*

[93] *Id.* at 3.

[94] *See* OFFICE OF THE PROSECUTOR, *supra* note 75, at 4. *See also* Rome Statute, Art. 8(2) (defining war crimes to include "intentionally directing attacks against the civilian population" and "intentionally launching an attack with knowledge that such attack will cause incidental loss ... which would be clearly excessive in relation to the concrete and direct overall military advantage anticipated).

[95] *See id. See also* Rome Statute, Arts. 8(2)(b)(i), 8(2)(b)(iv).

[96] OFFICE OF THE PROSECUTOR, *supra* note 75, at 6.

[97] *Id.*

[98] *Id.*

[99] *Id.*

[100] *Id.* at 7.

[101] OFFICE OF THE PROSECUTOR, *supra* note 75, at 7.

[102] *Id.*

[103] *Id.*

[104] *Id.*

[105] *Id.* at 9.

[106] OFFICE OF THE PROSECUTOR, *supra* note 75, at 9.

[107] *Id.*

[108] *Id.*

[109] Louis Charbonneau, *ICC Prosecutor Eyes Possible Afghanistan War Crimes*, REUTERS, Sept. 9, 2009, http://www.reuters.com/article/idUSTRE58871K20090909; LUCIA DICICCO, THE AMERICAN NON-GOVERNMENTAL ORGANIZATION, COMMUNICATIONS TO THE ICC REGARDING THE SITUATION IN AFGHANISTAN 1 (Sept. 14, 2009), http://www.amicc.org/docs/Afghanistan.pdf. The Reuters article summarizes three sets of allegations that could be under consideration, depending on the information the Prosecutor received: (1) Afghan officials' allegations that "unwarranted NATO air strikes" have caused "heavy civilian death tolls;" (2) NATO officials' allegations that the Taliban and al Qaeda are guilty of "attacking schools and kidnapping and murdering aid workers and other innocent civilians;" and (3) rights groups' accusations that the Bush Administration "authorized the use of torture in Afghan jails ..." *Id.*

[110] Charbonneau, *supra* note 109.

[111] Although it is not necessarily an indication of future behavior, the last time that the ICC considered allegations against U.S. troops, the Prosecutor did make public his decision not to initiate a formal investigation. That investigation would have looked into U.S. soldiers' activities in Iraq. The Prosecutor's decision and reasoning not to seek the Pre-Trial Chamber's authority to investigate is available on the ICC Office of the Prosecutor website.

[112] U.S. Congress, House Committee on Foreign Affairs, *U.S. Strategy in Afghanistan – Part II*, 111th Cong., 1st sess., Dec. 10, 2009.

[113] *See* Rome Statute, Art. 16. *E.g.* SC Res. 1422, U.N. Doc. S/RES/1422 (2002).

[114] Rome Statute, Art. 89(1).

[115] *See* Agreement Regarding the Surrender of Persons to the International Criminal Court, U.S.-Afg., Sept. 20, 2002, Temp. State Dep't No. 03-119, KAV 6308; Rome Statute, Art. 89.1 (indicating that only State Parties are required to comply with a request to surrender).

[116] Status of Military and Civilian Personnel, U.S.-Afg., Sept. 26, 2002–May 28, 2003 (entered into force May 28, 2003), Temp. State Dep't No. 03-67, KAV 6192. For more on the United States-Afghanistan SOFA, read the relevant portion of CRS Report RL34531, *Status of Forces Agreement (SOFA): What Is It, and How Has It Been Utilized?*, by R. Chuck Mason.

[117] *See* Article 98(2).

[118] *See* Prost & Kreß, *supra* note 54, at 1614. However, these agreements would not block the ICC from requesting a country without a BIA with the United States to extradite the American suspect if the suspect came on to its territory. *See* Agreement Regarding the Surrender of Persons to the International Criminal Court, U.S.-Afg., Aug. 23, 2003, Temp. State Dep't No. 03-119, KAV 6308; Rome Statute, Art. 89.1 (indicating that only State Parties are required to comply with a request to surrender).

[119] *See supra* notes 55-65 and accompanying text. This discussion pointed to three common perspectives on what agreements contained obligations that Article 98 was drafted to protect: (1) obligations contained in agreements that protect persons present on the foreign territory because they were sent there on official business (the prototype of these agreements are Status of Forces Agreements (SOFAs) like the one between the United States and Afghanistan), (2) obligations contained in agreements that were entered into by the State Party before it signed the Rome Statute (which may include the U.S.-Afghanistan BIA since it was signed before Afghanistan signed the Rome Statute), and (3) obligations contained in any international agreement no matter its label or the date it entered force (a perspective that would include both the United States-Afghanistan BIA and SOFA).

[120] Under this approach, the key to having the ICC respect the U.S.-Afghanistan BIA would, arguably, be the scope of its protection against extradition: only if its protection is limited to U.S citizens sent to Afghanistan on official business would Article 98 permit the agreement to preempt a request to surrender. The BIA prohibits the United States and Afghanistan from surrendering to the ICC the "persons" of either party, meaning any "current or former Government officials, employees (including contractors), or military personnel or *nationals of one Party*." Agreement Regarding the Surrender of Persons to the International Criminal Court, U.S.-Afg., Sept. 20, 2002, Temp. State Dep't No. 03-119, KAV 6308 (emphasis added). Therefore, if the ICC adopted this approach, it might read the BIA as extending protection against extradition to too broad a range of people to warrant preservation under Article 98. However, under this same approach, the ICC might conclude that the *SOFA* preempts an ICC request to Afghanistan for the surrender of U.S. personnel because it contains the type of obligations that proponents of this view believe Article 98 was intended to preserve. *See* Status of Military and Civilian Personnel, U.S.-Afg., Sept. 26, 2002–May 28, 2003 (entered into force May 28, 2003), Temp. State Dep't No. 03-67, KAV 6192 (prohibiting Afghanistan from surrendering or otherwise transferring "United States personnel" to the custody of an international tribunal, other entity, or other state without the express consent of the U.S. government).

[121] Under the approach that Article 98 preserves only those international obligations contained in agreements that Afghanistan signed before it signed the Rome Statute on February 10, 2003, the BIA would most likely preempted an ICC request for the surrender of a U.S. national because it was signed on September 20, 2002, several months before Afghanistan signed the Rome Statute. *See supra* notes 61-65 and accompanying text.

[122] Under the textualist approach on which United States has relied in creating BIAs, Article 98 preserves all BIAs, regardless of the scope of their protection against extradition or date on which they were signed, because a State Party's compliance with an ICC request to surrender necessitates its non-compliance with a BIA.

[123] *See* Prost & Kreß, *supra* note 54, at 1616. As Prost and Kreß describe the issue, "[A]ny determination by the Court that no conflicting international obligation exists will leave the requested State Party with the risk that the Court's determination of the international legal obligation is wrong. It was felt, however, that this risk is a tolerable one to bear in light of both the judicial expertise united on the bench and the persuasive authority that any relevant determination by the Court is bound to carry with it." *Id.*

[124] OFFICE OF THE PROSECUTOR, *supra* note 78.

[125] Palestine was not represented by a delegation at the Rome Conference but was able to send an observer delegation to the talks. COALITION FOR THE INTERNATIONAL CRIMINAL COURT, THE ICC AND THE ARAB WORLD 1 (2009), *available at* http://www.iccnow.org/documents/Arab_States_the_ICC_Factsheet__EN_.pdf.

[126] *See* Rome Statute, Art. 4(2) ("The Court may exercise its functions and powers ... on the territory of any State Party and, by special agreement, on the territory of any other *State*." (emphasis added)). In light of this complication, the Minister of Justice of the Palestinian National Authority (PNA), Dr. Ali Khashan, has also submitted legal arguments in support of its declaration. Press Release, ICC, ICC Prosecutor Receives Palestinian Minister of Justice, Arab League, and Independent Fact-Finding Committee (Oct. 16, 2009) *available at* http://www.icc-cpi.int/Menus/ICC/Press+and+Media/Press+Releases/Press+Releases +%282009%29/ (last visited Mar. 5, 2010).

[127] *E.g.* Joshua Rozenberg, *ICC's Credibility Hangs on Palestinian Statehood Decision*, Law Soc'y Gazette, May 21, 2009. However, the question would evade being answered by either

the Prosecutor or the ICC if the U.N. Security Council referred the situation to the ICC. *See* Rome Statute, Art. 13(b); *see also* John Quigley, *The Palestine Declaration to the International Criminal Court: The Statehood Issue*, 35 RUTGERS L. REC. 1, 9 (2009) (stating that, other than conferral of jurisdiction by the PNA's declaration, the only other potential bases for ICC jurisdiction over these allegations would be the nationality of a particular offender or a referral by the Security Council).

[128] OFFICE OF THE PROSECUTOR, *supra* note 78.

[129] OFFICE OF THE PROSECUTOR, INTERNATIONAL CRIMINAL COURT, VISIT OF THE PALESTINIAN NATIONAL AUTHORITY MINISTER OF FOREIGN AFFAIRS, MR. RIAD AL-MALKI, AND MINISTER OF JUSTICE, MR. ALI KHASHAN, TO THE PROSECUTOR OF THE ICC (Feb. 13, 2009), http://www.icc-pi.int/Menus/ICC/Structure+of+the+Court/Office+of+the+Prosecutor/Comm+and+Ref/Palestine (follow "Visit of the Minister of Justice of the Palestinian National Authority") (last visited Dec. 14, 2009).

[130] For an in-depth discussion of the conflict, see CRS Report R40101, *Israel and Hamas: Conflict in Gaza (2008-2009)*, coordinated by Jim Zanotti.

[131] The text is available at http://www2.ohchr.org/english/bodies/hrcouncil/docs/12session/A-HRC-12-48.pdf.

[132] COALITION FOR THE INTERNATIONAL CRIMINAL COURT, THE ICC AND THE ARAB WORLD 3 (2009), *available at* http://www.iccnow.org/documents/ Arab_ States_ the_ICC_Factsheet__EN_.pdf.

[133] *Id.*

[134] *See* Rome Statute, Art. 13(b). However, if the U.N. Security Council grants the ICC jurisdiction over the case, the ICC Prosecutor will still be required to conduct a preliminary analysis and address any issues of admissibility.

[135] SC Res. 1593, U.N. Doc S/RES/1593 (2005).

[136] The text of the U.N.HRC resolution (Resolution S-12/1), dated October 16, 2009, is available at http://www2.ohchr.org/english/bodies/hrcouncil/docs/12session/A-HRC-12-48.pdf.

[137] Remarks by State Department Spokesman Ian Kelly, September 19, 2008, http://www. state. gov/r/pa/prs/ps/2009/sept/129371.htm.

[138] *See e.g.* Remarks by Ambassador Alejandro Wolff, U.S. Deputy Permanent Representative to the United Nations, on the Middle East, at the Security Council Stakeout, October 7, 2009, http://usun.state.gov/briefing/statements/2009/130384.htm; Remarks by State Department Spokesman Ian Kelly, October 8, 2009.

[139] Quotation as reported by several news organizations. *See e.g.* Tom Maliti, *Envoy says US to Attend War Crimes Court Meeting*, ASSOCIATED PRESS ONLINE, Nov. 16, 2009; *US to Resume Engagement With ICC*, BBC NEWS, Nov. 16, 2009, http://news.bbc.co.uk /2/hi/8363282.stm; *Kenya Said to Give Shelter to Financier of Rwanda Genocide*, VOICE OF AMERICA, Nov. 16, 2009, http://www1.voanews.com/english/news/a-13-2009-11-16-voa52-70423427.html.

[140] Colum Lynch, *US to Attend, but Not Join, ICC Conference*, WASH. POST, Nov. 17, 2009, p. A20.

[141] Quotation as reported by several news organizations. *See e.g,* Maliti, *supra* note 120; David Clarke, *U.S. to Attend Hague Court Meeting as Observer*, REUTERS, Nov. 16, 2009.

[142] Stephen J. Rapp, U.S. Ambassador-at-Large for War Crimes Issues, *Remarks to the 2009 ICC Assembly of States Parties*, Nov. 19, 2009.

[143] *Id.*

[144] *Id.*

[145] Ambassador Rosemary A. DiCarlo, U.S. Alternate Representative to the United Nations for Special Political Affairs, *Remarks in the Security Council Chamber on Sudan and the ICC*, Dec. 4, 2009.

[146] Lynch, *supra* note 140.

[147] Rapp, *supra* note 142.

[148] See David Scheffer, *The Security Council's Struggle Over Darfur and International Justice*, *JURIST*, Aug. 20, 2008, http://jurist.law.pitt.edu/forumy/2008/08/security-councils-struggle-over-darfur.php.

[149] James B. Warlick, Assistant Secretary of State for International Organization Affairs, *U.S. Reengagement With the U.N.*, U.S. Department of State Foreign Press Center Briefing, Mar. 30, 2009; National Public Radio, Interview With Susan E. Rice, U.S. Ambassador to the United Nations, Mar. 6, 2009; Colum Lynch, *Sudan Retains Clout While Charges Loom*, WASH. POST, Feb. 9, 2009.

[150] Susan E. Rice, U.S. Ambassador to the United Nations, press release concerning issuance of ICC warrant for arrest of President Omar Hassan Ahmad al-Bashir of Sudan, Mar. 4, 2009, http://www.usunnewyork.usmission.gov/press_releases/20090304_039.html.

[151] Ambassador Rapp, responding to a question concerning the arrest warrant for Sudanese President al-Bashir, stated that "we will support efforts of the ICC to enforce its arrest warrant." U.S. Congress, Senate Committee on Foreign Relations, hearing to consider nominations, 111th Cong., 1st sess., July 22, 2009 (text from *Federal News Service*; available from LexisNexis Congressional; accessed 3/10/2010).

[152] U.S. Department of State, "U.S. "Ready to Lead Once More" at United Nations," *America.gov*, Aug. 14, 2009; Susan E. Rice, U.S. Ambassador to the United Nations, *A New Course in the World, a New Approach at the U.N.*, remarks at New York University's Center for Global Affairs and Center on International Cooperation, Aug. 12, 2009.

[153] SC Res. 1888, U.N. Doc. S/RES/1888 (2009).

[154] Rapp, *supra* note 142.

[155] See Hillary Clinton, written responses to questions for the record from Sen. John Kerry in advance of nomination hearing to become Secretary of State, January 2009, p. 66, http://www.amicc.org/docs/KerryClintonQFRs.pdf.

[156] *Id.* The ICC has thus far instituted proceedings for cases originating solely in sub-Saharan Africa (although it has conducted an investigation of paramilitaries in Colombia). For a detailed discussion of the ICC cases in Africa, see CRS Report RL34665, *International Criminal Court Cases in Africa: Status and Policy Issues*, by Alexis Arieff, Rhoda Margesson, and Marjorie Ann Browne.

[157] Ambassador Susan E. Rice, U.S. Permanent Representative to the United Nations, statement before the U.N. Security Council, Jan. 29, 2009.

[158] Secretary of State Hillary Clinton, *Remarks at "Townterview" Hosted by CNN and KTN*, University of Nairobi, Nairobi, Kenya, Aug. 6, 2009, http://www.state.gov/ secretary / rm /2009a/08/126954.htm.

[159] Nomination Hearing, *supra* note 151.

[160] Ambassador Rapp served as a prosecutor for two special courts, namely the International Criminal Tribunal for Rwanda and the Special Court for Sierra Leone.

[161] Secretary of State Clinton Delivers Remarks with Kenyan Foreign Minister Moses Wetangula, CQ Transcripts, August 5, 2009.

[162] See Remarks of U.S. Ambassador Michael Ranneberger to the Law Society of Kenya, "The Reform Agenda and Kenya's Historic Opportunity," October 30, 2009, http://nairobi.usembassy.gov/root/pdfs/reformag.pdf.

[163] U.S. Embassy Nairobi, "Ambassador Ranneberger Discusses U.S.-Kenyan Relations," CO. NX webchat transcript, August 12, 2009, http://nairobi.usembassy. gov/root/ pdfs/ transcript 090812.pdf.

[164] Remarks by Ambassador Susan Rice on Women, Peace and Security, USU.N. Press Release, August 7, 2009, http://www.america.gov/st/democracyhr-english/2009/August /200908 07170949eaifas0.2164074.html.

[165] Nomination Hearing, *supra* note 151.

[166] *Id.*

[167] Formerly codified at 22 U.S.C. § 7426.

[168] The current major non-NATO allies (MNNAs) are Argentina, Australia, Bahrain, Egypt, Israel, Japan, Jordan, Kuwait, Morocco, New Zealand, Pakistan, the Philippines, Thailand, and the Republic of Korea. 22 C.F.R. § 120.32.

[169] Former Representative George Nethercutt first proposed an amendment to the Foreign Operations, Export Financing, and Related Programs Appropriations Act, 2005 containing the original provision prohibiting ESF assistance to ICC States Parties.

[170] This provision applied to continuing appropriations made in FY2008.

[171] Compare Section 2007(b) of ASPA, which provided for a waiver under a determination of national interest, not national *security* interest (emphasis not in legislation). In addition, under Section 574, NATO members, MNNAs, and Taiwan may be eligible for waiver, but are not outright exempt from the prohibition.

In: International Criminal Court
Editor: Michael N. Baker
ISBN: 978-1-61324-694-8

Chapter 4

INTERNATIONAL CRIMINAL COURT REVIEW CONFERENCE KAMPALA, UGANDA*

Committee on Foreign Relations, U.S. Senate

May 31–June 11, 2010

COMMITTEE ON FOREIGN RELATIONS

John F. Kerry, Massachusetts, *Chairman*
Christopher J. Dodd, Connecticut
Russell D. Feingold, Wisconsin
Barbara Boxer, California
Robert Menendez, New Jersey
Benjamin L. Cardin, Maryland
Robert P. Casey, JR., Pennsylvania
Jim Webb, Virginia
Jeanne Shaheen, New Hampshire
Edward E. Kaufman, Delaware
Kirsten E. Gillibrand, New York
Richard G. Lugar, Indiana
Bob Corker, Tennessee
Johnny Isakson, Georgia

* This is an edited, reformatted and augmented version of a A Joint Committee Staff Trip Report publication, Prepared for Use of the Committee on Foreign Relations United States Senate, dated September 2, 2010.

James E. Risch, Idaho
Jim Demint, South Carolina
John Barrasso, Wyoming
Roger F. Wicker, Mississippi
James M. Inhofe, Oklahoma

Frank G. Lowenstein,
Staff Director

Kenneth A. Myers, Jr.,
Republican Staff Director

LETTER OF TRANSMITTAL

United states senate, committee on foreign relations,
Washington, DC, September 2, 2010.

Dear colleagues: In May 2010, we directed two members of the Foreign Relations Committee staff, Minority Chief Counsel Michael Mattler and Majority Deputy Chief Counsel Andrew Keller, to observe U.S. participation at the Review Conference of the Rome Statute of the International Criminal Court (ICC), which took place in Kampala, Uganda, from May 31–June 11, 2010. The conference represented the first time parties to the ICC considered amendments to the Rome Statute since it entered into force in 2002. We thank the co-heads of the U.S. delegation, State Department Legal Adviser Harold Koh and Ambassador at Large for War Crimes Issues Stephen Rapp, along with their colleagues from the Departments of State, Defense, and Justice, for including Mr. Mattler and Mr. Keller as part of the U.S. delegation.

The United States is not a party to the ICC, and is unlikely to become a party anytime soon. Nonetheless, the United States had interests at stake in the discussions at Kampala. The principal focus of the Kampala Conference was consideration of proposals to add to the ICC's jurisdiction a new crime of aggression, some of which could have seriously affected uses of military force by the United States and its allies. The United States also had an interest in better understanding the state of the ICC's work generally, and its prospects for making an effective contribution to promoting accountability for genocide, war crimes, and crimes against humanity. In this regard, the United States, under both the George W. Bush and Obama administrations, has supported the

ICC's investigation of such crimes in Darfur, pursuant to a 2005 referral by the U.N. Security Council.

As this report highlights, the Kampala Conference adopted a complicated decision that envisions the future addition of a crime of aggression to the ICC's jurisdiction. The proposed aggression regime is flawed in several respects, but nonetheless contains important protections for U.S. interests. Most significantly, U.S. persons, including U.S. officials and military members, could not be investigated or prosecuted for aggression by the ICC without the consent of the United States. The proposed regime will not enter into force for at least seven years, and will do so only after a further decision by the ICC's parties to bring it into force. U.S. participation at the Kampala Conference played an important role in securing these protections.

The report also observes that, with the Conference's focus on adding a new crime to the ICC's mandate, ICC parties spent comparatively little energy at the Conference addressing a range of operational challenges currently faced by the Court. Eight years after entering into force, the ICC has yet to complete its first trial and is encountering a variety of practical obstacles to its effectiveness. Absent greater focus on addressing such difficulties in the ICC's operations, the court may continue to struggle in carrying out its basic judicial functions.

We hope you find this report useful and informative. We welcome any comments you may have on it.

Sincerely,
John f. Kerry,
Chairman.

Richard g. Lugar,
Ranking minority member

Background

The International Criminal Court was established in 1998. Under the treaty establishing the ICC, known as the Rome Statute, the Court has jurisdiction to investigate and prosecute cases of genocide, war crimes, and crimes against humanity. The treaty entered into force in 2002 and currently has 113 states parties. The United States is not a party to the ICC.

On May 31, 2010, the parties to the ICC convened a 2-week conference to assess the work of the ICC since its inception and to consider amendments to the Rome Statute. The United States sent a delegation to the conference and participated as an observer.

The principal issue before the conference was whether to amend the Rome Statute to add a new crime aggression to the ICC's jurisdiction. The conference also considered two more technical amendments to the statute, and held a series of moderated discussions to take stock of elements of the ICC's performance to date. The stocktaking discussions addressed the relationship between the court's work and broader efforts to resolve conflict and restore peace, the impact of the court's work on victims of crimes, the extent of cooperation with the court by states, and efforts by states to establish accountability for serious crimes at the national level. This report addresses the Conference's discussions and decisions related to the crime of aggression.

Pre-Conference Discussions of Aggression

As adopted in 1998, the Rome Statute gave the ICC jurisdiction over three crimes: genocide, war crimes, and crimes against humanity. At the Rome Conference, negotiators discussed giving the court jurisdiction over the additional crime of aggression, but were unable to agree on a definition of the crime or on the conditions under which the ICC might exercise jurisdiction over it. As a compromise, the Rome Statute provided that the ICC could exercise jurisdiction over aggression in the future if the statute were amended to address these issues.

Following the Rome Conference, the ICC's Assembly of States Parties established a special working group on the crime of aggression. The working group met between 2003 and 2009 and developed proposals on both a definition of the crime aggression and on conditions under which the ICC might exercise jurisdiction over it. The United States did not participate in the working group. The working group's proposals are described briefly below.

Definition of Aggression—In contrast to the other crimes within the ICC's jurisdiction, aggression has not previously been widely employed as a criminal law concept in domestic or international law. In the aftermath of World War II, the International Military Tribunals in Nuremburg and Tokyo prosecuted a few German and Japanese officials for "crimes against peace," though there was no widely agreed definition of this concept prior to the war. Following the war, the U.N. Charter gave the Security Council the authority to determine when a state had committed an "act of aggression" and to decide on measures to be taken to restore international peace and security. But the Charter's treatment of aggression does not provide for criminal liability on the part of individuals.

The working group recommended a definition based largely on a 1974 U.N. General Assembly resolution, which was adopted for the purpose of providing guidance to the U.N. Security Council's use in determining whether a state had committed aggression for the purposes of the U.N. Charter. The working group's definition reads as follows:

Article 8 Bis—Crime of Aggression

1) For the purpose of this Statute, "crime of aggression" means the planning, preparation, initiation or execution, by a person in a position effectively to exercise control over or to direct the political or military action of a State, of an act of aggression which, by its character, gravity and scale, constitutes a manifest violation of the Charter of the United Nations.
2) For the purpose of paragraph 1, "act of aggression" means the use of armed force by a State against the sovereignty, territorial integrity or political independence of another State, or in any other manner inconsistent with the Charter of the United Nations. Any of the following acts, regardless of a declaration of war, shall, in accordance with United Nations General Assembly resolution 3314 (XXIX) of 14 December 1974, qualify as an act of aggression:

   a) The invasion or attack by the armed forces of a State of the territory of another State, or any military occupation, however temporary, resulting from such invasion or attack, or any annexation by the use of force of the territory of another State or part thereof;
   b) Bombardment by the armed forces of a State against the territory of another State or the use of any weapons by a State against the territory of another State;
   c) The blockade of the ports or coasts of a State by the armed forces of another State;

d) An attack by the armed forces of a State on the land, sea or air forces, or marine and air fleets of another State;
e) The use of armed forces of one State which are within the territory of another State with the agreement of the receiving State, in contravention of the conditions provided for in the agreement or any extension of their presence in such territory beyond the termination of the agreement;
f) The action of a State in allowing its territory, which it has placed at the disposal of another State, to be used by that other State for perpetrating an act of aggression against a third State;
g) The sending by or on behalf of a State of armed bands, groups, irregulars or mercenaries, which carry out acts of armed force against another State of such gravity as to amount to the acts listed above, or its substantial involvement therein.

Three key elements are at the core of the proposed definition: First, aggression is a crime committed by political or military leaders such as heads of state or senior military officials who, on behalf of a state, plan or direct acts of aggression carried out by others. Aggression is not committed by officials or soldiers carrying out the decisions of others.

Second, aggression involves the use of force in violation of the U.N. Charter. Under the U.N. Charter, states are prohibited from using force against the territorial integrity or political independence of another state except in self-defense from an armed attack or if authorized by the U.N. Security Council.

Third, aggression arises only in the case of "manifest" violations of the U.N. Charter, meaning that the character, gravity, and scale of the violation are clearly established.

Conditions for the Exercise of Jurisdiction Over Aggression—The working group was unable to arrive at a consensus recommendation regarding the conditions under which the ICC might exercise jurisdiction over aggression. Delegations fell broadly into two camps on this issue.

Permanent members of the U.N. Security Council took the position that the ICC should exercise jurisdiction over aggression only in cases in which the U.N. Security Council had specifically asked it to do so. The U.N. Charter vests the Security Council with the responsibility for determining the existence of an act of aggression, and measures to be taken to maintain or restore international peace and security. An independent role for the ICC in investigating and prosecuting aggression could prejudice the Council's efforts to resolve situations involving potential aggression and create the risk of broader conflict.

Most other countries supported some authority for the ICC to exercise jurisdiction over aggression independently of the U.N. Security Council. These countries were concerned that a deadlock in the Security Council over a particular case would prevent the ICC from being able to address a case of aggression. They also argued that the Security Council's involvement in deciding whether cases could proceed would inject political considerations into judicial matters and undermine the integrity of the ICC's proceedings.

HISTORICAL U.S. POSITION ON AGGRESSION

While the United States did not participate in the work of the Assembly of States Parties' special working group on aggression, the United States has historically expressed concerns about proposals to include aggression within the ICC's jurisdiction.

In 1998 testimony before the Senate Foreign Relations Committee, the Clinton administration's chief negotiator at the Rome Conference, David Scheffer, expressed the following set of concerns about the treatment of aggression in the original Rome Statute:

We are disappointed with the treatment of the crime of aggression. We and others had long argued that such a crime had not been defined under customary international law for purposes of individual criminal responsibility. We also insisted, as did the International Law Commission in 1994, that there had to be a direct linkage between a prior Security Council decision that a state had committed aggression and the conduct of an individual of that state. The statute of the court now includes a crime of aggression, but leaves it to be defined by a subsequent amendment to be adopted 7 years after entry into force. There is no guarantee that the vital linkage with a prior decision by the Security Council will be required by the definition that emerges, if in fact a broadly acceptable definition can be achieved. We will do all we can to ensure that such linkage survives.[1]

This statement reflected two principal concerns at the heart of the U.S. position:

First, the United States has expressed concerns that aggression has not been sufficiently defined to form an appropriate basis for criminal prosecutions. Prosecutions based on a definition of aggression that does not reflect customary international law would create the risk that individuals could face criminal penalties for uses of force that have not traditionally been considered unlawful by the international community. This could serve to discourage a wider range of uses of force than are prohibited under existing customary international law, including some that may be necessary to protect the security interests of the United States and its allies. In addition, in the absence of a clear and accepted definition of the crime, potential defendants would not have clear guidance about what actions are prohibited, raising fundamental questions of fairness and due process in any criminal proceedings.

Second, the United States has expressed concerns about the potential impact of an ICC crime of aggression on the role and authority of the U.N. Security Council. As a permanent member of the Security Council, the United States has an interest in ensuring that actions by the ICC in relation to alleged cases of aggression do not interfere with the Council's own efforts to address matters of international peace and security.

In addition to these considerations, U.S. policy has also stressed a strong interest in protecting U.S. persons, including U.S. officials and members of the armed forces, against potential ICC investigations or prosecutions for aggression, which may be unfounded or politically motivated. As a nonparty to the ICC, the United States has long objected to any efforts by the ICC to assert jurisdiction over Americans with respect to its core crimes of genocide, war crimes, and crimes against humanity. Securing protections against such assertions of jurisdiction by the ICC was a core objective of the American Servicemembers' Protection Act, passed by Congress in 2002.[2] Concerns about U.S. exposure to an ICC regime for aggression would be especially acute, given that aggression cases would involve potential criminal prosecution of the President and other senior political and military leaders for their decisions and actions related to matters of U.S. national security.

THE OBAMA ADMINISTRATION'S APPROACH TO THE KAMPALA CONFERENCE

The administration's decision to attend the Kampala Conference as an observer reflected two principal considerations. First, the administration sought to address U.S. concerns and protect U.S. interests with respect to the proposed ICC aggression regime, including those discussed above. Second, the administration sought to ex accountability for international crimes such as genocide, crimes against humanity, and war crimes. This included exploring ways in which the United States, as a nonparty to the ICC, could work with ICC members to advance shared objectives in this area.

Consistent with these objectives, the United States delegation in Kampala raised a series of concerns in connection with the conference's consideration of the crime of aggression. These concerns fell into four main categories:

Concerns With the Content of the Definition—The U.S. delegation observed that the proposed aggression definition was vague in a number of respects, creating uncertainty on several important issues. They noted that the proposed definition applied to "acts of aggression" rather than "wars of aggression" that were the subject of prosecution at Nuremburg, leaving unclear the scope of the crime. They also noted that it was unclear how the term "manifest" in the definition would apply, including whether it must be shown that a state was "manifestly" not acting in self-defense or with the consent of the state where force was used. It was also unclear how the "manifest" standard would apply in cases where force was used for the purpose of preventing serious crimes such as genocide, war crimes, and crimes against humanity. The U.S. delegation also noted ways in which the definition departed from existing customary international law, as well as from the General Assembly Resolution on which the definition was based. These included the definition's failure to specify that only the most serious and dangerous forms of illegal uses of force constitute aggression, with the determination whether an act of aggression has occurred requiring careful consideration of the circumstances of each particular case, including the purpose for which force was used.

Concerns With the Conditions for the Exercise of Jurisdiction Over Aggression—Consistent with the historical U.S. position, the U.S. delegation took the position that a prior decision of the U.N. Security Council that aggression had occurred should be a precondition to the ICC's exercise of jurisdiction over the crime of aggression in any case. The delegation opposed proposals for alternative jurisdictional schemes in which the ICC could exercise jurisdiction over aggression without prior Security Council approval, including proposals in which the ICC Prosecutor could proceed with cases after a period of notice to the Security Council unless the Council affirmatively decided that the case should not proceed. The U.S. delegation also stressed longstanding U.S. concerns about any effort to subject states to ICC jurisdiction over aggression without their consent, except in cases of referral by the U.N. Security Council.

Concerns With the Impact of the ICC's Aggression Regime for National Justice Systems—The U.S. delegation expressed concern that adding aggression to the Rome Statute could lead to efforts by individual states to prosecute leaders of other countries for aggression through their national courts. This risk arises because, under the Rome Statute, the ICC is a court of last resort and may exercise jurisdiction over a crime only where relevant states are unwilling or unable to investigate and prosecute them through their national justice systems. Under this system, states are encouraged to prosecute crimes domestically rather than requiring recourse to the ICC. The U.S. delegation expressed concerns that encouraging domestic prosecutions of aggression, which could involve two countries to a conflict each trying to prosecute the other's leaders in its own courts, could exacerbate tensions and undermine international peace and security.

Concerns With the Process for Making Decisions About Aggression—In light of the divergent views over the circumstances in which the ICC might exercise jurisdiction over aggression, the U.S. delegation also stressed the importance that any decisions be based on a consensus among ICC members (which would necessarily include the United Kingdom and France, which are permanent members of the U.N. Security Council). The U.S. delegation observed that all prior Rome Statute crimes had been adopted by consensus and that adoption of a regime for the politically charged crime of aggression over the objections of some countries would undermine the legitimacy of both the crime and the ICC itself.

Discussions on Aggression at the Kampala Conference

The negotiations at the Kampala Conference focused on four principal issues: the content of the definition of aggression, the conditions for the exercise of jurisdiction over aggression, whether the aggression regime would apply to states that had not consented to it, and the process for adopting amendments to the Rome Statute regarding aggression.

Content of the Definition—In spite of U.S. criticism of the definition of the crime of aggression proposed by the Assembly of States Parties' special working group, the definition itself was widely supported at the conference, including by U.S. allies such as the United Kingdom and France. This support did not appear to be based on substantive disagreement with the questions raised by the United States about the definition. Instead, it seemed to reflect concern that reopening the definition would delay the process of reaching a final decision on aggression (to which many countries were firmly committed) and that other compromises that had been made in arriving at the proposed definition might be revisited if the text were reconsidered.

While the Conference was accordingly unwilling to entertain changes to the definition's text, delegations were willing to discuss adopting "understandings" addressing elements of the definition. Such understandings were viewed as a means of providing authoritative guidance to the ICC Prosecutor and judges on interpretive issues related to the definition. The United States proposed a series of understandings to address concerns it had raised about the definition. These included understandings designed to provide greater clarity about the meaning of a "manifest" violation of the U.N. Charter as used in the definition, to specify that an ICC aggression regime would not create the right or obligation for states to exercise domestic jurisdiction over alleged acts of aggression by other states, and to provide greater specificity about the level of gravity required to establish the existence of aggression.

Conditions for the Exercise of Jurisdiction—This represented the most contentious issue of the conference. Most delegations opposed the position of the five permanent members of the Security Council that the ICC Prosecutor should have authority to investigate and prosecute aggression only in cases where the Council had previously determined that a state had committed an act of aggression. This majority view reflected a concern that the ICC's judicial role required it to operate independently from political constraints. It also reflected deep dissatisfaction with the Security Council among developing countries, and concern that Security Council decisions would reflect the interests of the five permanent members rather than the interests of the international community as a whole.

Most delegations proposed giving the Security Council at most a fixed period of time to determine whether a state had committed aggression in connection with a situation in which the ICC Prosecutor wished to investigate or prosecute an individual for aggression. In the absence of a determination by the Security Council by the end of the time period, these countries urged that the Prosecutor have the authority to move forward with the case on his own initiative.

Consent Requirement—Delegations differed over whether a state must have consented to the ICC's aggression jurisdiction in order for its nationals to be subject to investigation and prosecution for aggression by the ICC. States were more divided on this question than on the question related to the role of the Security Council. In general most countries, particularly those in the developing world, opposed a requirement that a state consent before an aggression regime would apply to its nationals. They argued that prosecutions for aggression would be less likely, and the deterrent created by the regime less effective, if it applied only to states that had consented. A sizeable minority, including a number of European countries, supported a consent requirement, arguing that such consent is a basic requirement to bind a state under international law. All delegations agreed that no state consent would be required where the ICC was prosecuting aggression at the request of the U.N. Security Council, which has the authority to bind U.N. member states pursuant to the U.N. Charter.

Process for Adopting Amendments Related to Aggression—Delegations also differed over the correct process for amending the Rome Statute to address aggression. At issue in the debate were two alternative methods provided for under the Rome Statute for adopting amendments. Under the first method, contained in Article 121, paragraph 4, amendments are binding on all Rome Statute parties once they have been approved by 7⁄8 of the states parties. Under the second method, contained in Article 121, paragraph 5, amendments are binding only on those states that have accepted them.

Delegations' positions on these procedural questions often mirrored their positions on whether state consent should be required for the ICC to have jurisdiction over the state's nationals. States opposed to a consent requirement tended to favor an amendment process that would bind all states so that an aggression regime could apply universally even if a minority of states objected to it and declined to ratify it. Supporters of a consent requirement generally supported an amendment process in which amendments would apply only to those states that ratified them, so that non-ratifying states could avoid being bound by a regime that was adopted over their objections.

OUTCOME

Discussions at the Kampala Conference were unable to fully resolve the most contentious issues related to the proposed aggression regime. The Conference adopted a complicated decision that reflected compromises on several key issues. The decision provides that the envisioned aggression regime will not become operational for at least seven years, and even then only after a further decision by the ICC's Assembly of States Parties to bring it into effect. The text of the decision is attached as an annex to this report. Below is a summary of the key provisions of the decision:

Definition of Aggression—The Conference adopted the definition of aggression proposed by the Working Group without any amendment. In an effort to address concerns raised by the U.S. delegation about lack of clarity in aspects of the definition, the Conference adopted a series of interpretive understandings relating to aspects of the definition. Among the approved understandings were:

- An understanding specifying that, in assessing whether an act of aggression constitutes a "manifest" violation of the U.N. Charter, the character, gravity, and scale of the act must all be considered, and that no one of these elements by itself can satisfy the "manifest" standard;
- An understanding specifying that only the most serious and dangerous forms of the illegal use of force constitute aggression, and that determinations of aggression require considering all the relevant circumstances of each case, including the gravity of the acts and their consequences; and
- Two understandings specifying that the amendments address the crime of aggression only for the purpose of the Rome Statute, and that they shall not be interpreted as creating the right or obligation for states to exercise domestic jurisdiction over alleged acts of aggression by other states.

Conditions for the Exercise of Jurisdiction Over Aggression—The Conference adopted two separate procedures for the ICC to exercise jurisdiction over aggression. Under the first, the Court could exercise jurisdiction in cases specifically referred to the ICC by the U.N. Security Council. Under the second, the Court could exercise jurisdiction when requested by a state in which aggression is alleged to have occurred, or when the ICC Prosecutor decides on his own initiative to pursue a case. In the latter two cases, before an investigation may commence, the ICC Prosecutor must consult the U.N. Security Council and may only proceed if the Council either determines that the case involves a situation in which a state has committed aggression or fails to make any determination on this question. Where the Council makes no determination, the Prosecutor must receive authorization from a Pre-Trial Chamber of ICC Judges before he may commence an investigation. Where the Prosecutor proceeds with an investigation in the absence of an affirmative Security Council determination that aggression has occurred, the Council may pass a resolution suspending the investigation for 1 year, and may renew such a suspension for subsequent periods.

Consent Requirement—The decision adopted by the Conference allows states parties to the ICC to decline to accept the ICC's jurisdiction over aggression in cases that have not been referred by the U.N. Security Council. Similarly, the decision also specifies that the ICC shall not exercise jurisdiction in respect of alleged aggression committed by the nationals or on the territories of states that are not parties to the ICC, except where referred by the U.N. Security Council. All states would be subject to the ICC's aggression jurisdiction in cases referred by the Security Council.

Procedure for Adopting Amendments and Entry into Force—The decision adopted by the Conference provides for the relevant amendments to the Rome Statute to be adopted under Article 121(5) of the Rome Statute, meaning that the amendments will apply only to those states parties to the Rome Statute that approve them and not to those that decline to ratify. In addition, the amendments establish two additional requirements before they may enter into force. First, they will apply only to acts of aggression committed one year after 30 states have ratified them. Second, the ICC won't exercise jurisdiction over aggression until a decision is taken by the ICC parties, no earlier than January 1, 2017, to bring the ICC's aggression regime into effect.

Analysis of Outcome

The Kampala Conference's outcome on aggression has implications for both the United States and the ICC. These are discussed below.

Implications for the United States

1. Exemption for Non-States Parties

The most significant aspect of the outcome for the United States is its elimination of any risk that U.S. officials will be subject to prosecution for aggression by the ICC absent U.S. consent. The decision of the Assembly of States Parties exempts from key aspects of the ICC's aggression jurisdiction actions committed by the nationals or on the territories of countries, including the United States, that are not parties to the ICC. Such nonparties could only be prosecuted by the ICC for aggression in cases referred by the U.N. Security Council; they could not be prosecuted solely at the request of another country or by the ICC Prosecutor on his own initiative. Because the United States is a permanent member of the U.N. Security Council and has a veto over its decisions, the Council could not refer an aggression case involving U.S. officials to the ICC over the objection of the United States.

With respect to other crimes in the ICC's jurisdiction genocide, war crimes, and crimes against humanity the Rome Statute purports to give the ICC authority to prosecute nationals of countries that are not parties to the ICC without approval of the Security Council. As a nonparty, the United States has strenuously objected to this claim, and it has been a source of significant friction between the United States and the ICC. The ICC's decision not to repeat its claim of jurisdiction over nationals of nonparties when designing its aggression regime avoids a reigniting of this contentious issue.

2. Potential Impact on Coalition Activities

Because many U.S. allies, including all NATO members except Turkey, are parties to the ICC, they would be potentially subject to the ICC's aggression jurisdiction once it is brought into effect. This could make some U.S. allies more hesitant to join with the United States in uses of force without clear U.N. Security Council approval, as was the case with the 1999 NATO military actions in Kosovo and the 2003 military action in Iraq.

Two elements of the outcome adopted could mitigate such risks. First, under the decision adopted, states parties to the ICC can opt out of the ICC's aggression jurisdiction for cases not referred by the U.N. Security Council. If U.S. allies exercised this right, they would not incur any greater risk of prosecution for aggression by the ICC than would the United States. Second, understandings adopted in connection with the definition seek to underscore that aggression constitutes only the most serious and dangerous forms of the illegal use of force, and applies only when the character, gravity, and scale of the illegal use of force is manifest. These understandings arguably narrow the circumstances in which the ICC might bring an aggression case, and may reduce the likelihood that coalition military activities would be considered aggression, particularly when undertaken to address threats to civilian populations or to regional or international peace and security.

3. Potential Adverse Development in Law Relating to Use of Force

The definition of the crime of aggression adopted by the Conference establishes vague standards that would govern important questions relating to the use of military force by states subject to the ICC's aggression regime. As noted by the U.S. delegation in Kampala, the definition adopted deviates from existing customary international law in a number of respects, and may serve inappropriately to discourage lawful uses of force. Interpretive understandings adopted in connection with the definition serve to mitigate some of its deficiencies, but the definition remains an unsound basis for addressing these issues. Were the definition to influence the future development of international law outside the context of the ICC, future U.S. leaders could face increased criticism in connection with some decisions regarding the use of force, including claims that their decisions amount to criminal conduct.

4. Potential Impact on the U.N. Security Council

The regime adopted by the Conference, if made operational and subscribed to by a large number of states, would provide the ICC with authority to investigate and prosecute cases of aggression without the affirmative approval of the Security Council. In particular cases, the ICC's pursuit of an aggression case against a head of state or other senior government official could complicate the Security Council's efforts to address an ongoing threat to peace and security. Accordingly, there is some potential that the proposed aggression regime could reduce the effectiveness of the Council's mechanisms for addressing situations that may be of concern to the United States.

5. Additional Time to Work for Improvements

Because the aggression regime will not go into effect for at least seven years, the United States will have opportunities to further address concerns not resolved by the outcome. It could seek greater clarity in the definition of aggression, either through changes to the definition or the elements of crimes accompanying it, or through further underunderstandings. It will also have the opportunity to consult with allies and to develop plans to mitigate risks an ICC aggression regime might pose to the ability to plan and carry out coalition military operations.

Implications for the ICC

1. Potential Politicization

The crime of aggression has a significant political character to it, involving judgments about the legitimacy of decisions by state leaders to use force in situations affecting their security interests. This subjective political aspect of the crime is compounded by the vagueness of aspects of the definition of aggression. The outcome, if brought into effect, will place the ICC Prosecutor at the center of such political questions by giving him the mandate to investigate and prosecute aggression on his own initiative or at the request of a state. There is a risk that the Prosecutor will be drawn into disputes between states, and that the Prosecutor's decisions to pursue or not pursue particular cases will be seen as taking sides in such disputes. Such perceptions could undermine the perceived objectivity and legitimacy of the ICC as a judicial institution.

2. Potential Overstretch

The ICC is currently struggling to carry out its current mandate of pursuing cases of genocide, war crimes, and crimes against humanity. Eight years after the Rome Statute entered into force, the ICC has gained custody of fewer than half of the 15 individuals against whom it has brought public charges for the core crimes of genocide, war crimes, and crimes against humanity, and it has yet to complete its first trial. Though the ICC will have at least 7 years to further build its capacities before an aggression regime could take effect, there nonetheless remains the risk that adding aggression to the Court's mandate will divert resources from core tasks and make the ICC less effective as an institution.

FURTHER OBSERVATIONS ON THE NEGOTIATION PROCESS

In addition to these issues specific to the outcome at Kampala, several other developments at the Conference may be of interest to the Foreign Relations Committee and to the Senate more generally:

1. Widespread Dissatisfaction with the U.N. Security Council

Much of the discussion at the conference focused on whether the ICC Prosecutor should be given the authority to initiate aggression investigations and prosecutions independently from the U.N. Security Council. Discussion on this issue in both formal and informal settings suggested widespread dissatisfaction with the Security Council, particularly among delegations from developing countries. These delegations appeared to perceive the Council as an unrepresentative body that does not regularly act in the interests of the international community as a whole. For some delegations, pursuing outcomes that appeared to challenge the Security Council's primacy in addressing aggression appeared to be an independent objective in the negotiations, separate from the goal of pursuing decisions that would strengthen the ICC or international justice. Should such challenges to the Security Council's role and authority become more widespread and arise in other contexts, the Council's effectiveness as an institution could be diminished.

2. Disparate Views among NATO Members

While a potential ICC aggression regime could impact NATO military operations, NATO delegations at the conference were not unified in their substantive views or in their approach to the negotiations. NATO members also differed in their views on the importance of giving the ICC jurisdiction over aggression at all, with some being vigorous supporters and others skeptical at best. Some NATO delegations were among the chief proponents of an ICC role for aggression independent of the U.N. Security Council, while others felt strongly that the ICC should act on aggression only when asked by the Security Council. It did not appear from the negotiations that NATO members, as a group, had a common understanding about the potential implications of various proposals on their operations. Because of the relationship of the crime of aggression to decisions to use force that are often taken collectively, better NATO coordination on these issues in the future would be prudent.

3. Effectiveness of U.S. Participation

U.S. participation at the conference was well-received, had a significant impact on the outcome and served to protect important U.S. interests. While there has been significant past friction between the United States and the ICC, and while the Obama administration has made clear that it does not support the United States becoming a party to the ICC, ICC parties nonetheless are welcoming of increased U.S. engagement with the ICC. Absent U.S. participation and engagement before and during the Kampala Conference, it is unlikely that the conference would have specifically exempted non-ICC parties from key portions of the proposed aggression regime. It is also unlikely that the conference would have adopted understandings to address ambiguities in aspects of the definition of aggression. While there were limits to the lengths ICC parties were willing to go to address U.S. concerns and interests there was no willingness, for example, to consider revising the definition of aggression itself ICC parties did accommodate United States concerns in important respects.

4. ICC Priorities

The Kampala Conference was the first high- level meeting of the ICC Assembly of States Parties since the Rome Statute was adopted in 1998. It is notable that the parties were concerned primarily with expanding the ICC's jurisdiction to cover an additional crime rather than with considering ways of improving its ability to address effectively the crimes currently in the Court's mandate. The Conference gave only passing consideration to important practical obstacles currently faced by the ICC, including securing cooperation from states with ICC orders, gaining custody of persons charged with crimes, protecting victims and witnesses, facilitating evidence sharing and other legal assistance from states, and improving the efficiency of trial proceedings. The choice by the ICC parties to focus on aggression rather than on developing solutions to these challenges suggests that the parties were more concerned with the symbol of adopting an aggression regime than with the substance of building an effective institution. Absent greater focus on addressing these operational difficulties, the ICC may continue to struggle in carrying out its basic judicial functions.

ANNEX. ICC REVIEW CONFERENCE DECISION ON AGGRESSION

Resolution RC/Res.6

Adopted at the 13th plenary meeting, on 11 June 2010, by consensus

RC/Res.6
The Crime of Aggression

The Review Conference,

Recalling paragraph 1 of article 12 of the Rome Statute,

Recalling paragraph 2 of article 5 of the Rome Statute,

Recalling also paragraph 7 of resolution F, adopted by the United Nations Diplomatic Conference of Plenipotentiaries on the Establishment of an International Criminal Court on 17 July 1998,

Recalling further resolution ICC-ASP/1/Res.1 on the continuity of work in respect of the crime of aggression, and *expressing its appreciation* to the Special Working Group on the Crime of Aggression for having elaborated proposals on a provision on the crime of aggression,

Taking note of resolution ICC-ASP/8/Res.6, by which the Assembly of States Parties forwarded proposals on a provision on the crime of aggression to the Review Conference for its consideration,

Resolved to activate the Court's jurisdiction over the crime of aggression as early as possible,

1. *Decides* to adopt, in accordance with article 5, paragraph 2, of the Rome Statute of the International Criminal Court (hereinafter: "the Statute") the amendments to the Statute contained in annex I of the present resolution, which are subject to ratification or acceptance and shall enter into force in accordance with article 121, paragraph 5; and notes that any State Party may lodge a declaration referred to in article 15 *bis* prior to ratification or acceptance;

2. *Also decides* to adopt the amendments to the Elements of Crimes contained in annex II of the present resolution;

3. *Also decides* to adopt the understandings regarding the interpretation of the above-mentioned amendments contained in annex III of the present resolution;

4. *Further decides* to review the amendments on the crime of aggression seven years after the beginning of the Court's exercise of jurisdiction;

5. *Calls upon* all States Parties to ratify or accept the amendments contained in annex I.

Annex I

Amendments to the Rome Statute of the International Criminal Court on the Crime of Aggression

1. Article 5, paragraph 2, of the Statute is deleted.

2. The following text is inserted after article 8 of the Statute:

Article 8 *bis*
Crime of aggression

1. For the purpose of this Statute, "crime of aggression" means the planning, preparation, initiation or execution, by a person in a position effectively to exercise control over or to direct the political or military action of a State, of an act of aggression which, by its character, gravity and scale, constitutes a manifest violation of the Charter of the United Nations.

2. For the purpose of paragraph 1, "act of aggression" means the use of armed force by a State against the sovereignty, territorial integrity or political independence of another State, or in any other manner inconsistent with the Charter of the United Nations. Any of the following acts, regardless of a declaration of war, shall, in accordance with United Nations General Assembly resolution 3314 (XXIX) of 14 December 1974, qualify as an act of aggression:

a) The invasion or attack by the armed forces of a State of the territory of another State, or any military occupation, however temporary, resulting from such invasion or attack, or any annexation by the use of force of the territory of another State or part thereof;

b) Bombardment by the armed forces of a State against the territory of another State or the use of any weapons by a State against the territory of another State;

c) The blockade of the ports or coasts of a State by the armed forces of another State;

d) An attack by the armed forces of a State on the land, sea or air forces, or marine and air fleets of another State;

e) The use of armed forces of one State which are within the territory of another State with the agreement of the receiving State, in contravention of the conditions provided for in the agreement or any extension of their presence in such territory beyond the termination of the agreement;

f) The action of a State in allowing its territory, which it has placed at the disposal of another State, to be used by that other State for perpetrating an act of aggression against a third State;

g) The sending by or on behalf of a State of armed bands, groups, irregulars or mercenaries, which carry out acts of armed force against another State of such gravity as to amount to the acts listed above, or its substantial involvement therein.

3. The following text is inserted after article 15 of the Statute:

Article 15 *bis*
Exercise of jurisdiction over the crime of aggression
(State referral, *proprio motu*)

1. The Court may exercise jurisdiction over the crime of aggression in accordance with article 13, paragraphs (a) and (c), subject to the provisions of this article.

2. The Court may exercise jurisdiction only with respect to crimes of aggression committed one year after the ratification or acceptance of the amendments by thirty States Parties.

3. The Court shall exercise jurisdiction over the crime of aggression in accordance with this article, subject to a decision to be taken after 1 January 2017 by the same majority of States Parties as is required for the adoption of an amendment to the Statute.

4. The Court may, in accordance with article 12, exercise jurisdiction over a crime of aggression, arising from an act of aggression committed by a State Party, unless that State Party has previously declared that it does not accept such jurisdiction by lodging a declaration with the Registrar. The withdrawal of such a declaration may be effected at any time and shall be considered by the State Party within three years.

5. In respect of a State that is not a party to this Statute, the Court shall not exercise its jurisdiction over the crime of aggression when committed by that State's nationals or on its territory.

6. Where the Prosecutor concludes that there is a reasonable basis to proceed with an investigation in respect of a crime of aggression, he or she shall first ascertain whether the Security Council has made a determination of an act of aggression committed by the State concerned. The Prosecutor shall notify the Secretary-General of the United Nations of the situation before the Court, including any relevant information and documents.

7. Where the Security Council has made such a determination, the Prosecutor may proceed with the investigation in respect of a crime of aggression.

8. Where no such determination is made within six months after the date of notification, the Prosecutor may proceed with the investigation in respect of a crime of aggression, provided that the Pre-Trial Division has authorized the commencement of the investigation in respect of a crime of aggression in accordance with the procedure contained in article 15, and the Security Council has not decided otherwise in accordance with article 16.

9. A determination of an act of aggression by an organ outside the Court shall be without prejudice to the Court's own findings under this Statute.

10. This article is without prejudice to the provisions relating to the exercise of jurisdiction with respect to other crimes referred to in article 5.

4. The following text is inserted after article 15 bis of the Statute:

Article 15 *ter*
Exercise of jurisdiction over the crime of aggression
(Security Council referral)

1. The Court may exercise jurisdiction over the crime of aggression in accordance with article 13, paragraph (b), subject to the provisions of this article.

2. The Court may exercise jurisdiction only with respect to crimes of aggression committed one year after the ratification or acceptance of the amendments by thirty States Parties.

3. The Court shall exercise jurisdiction over the crime of aggression in accordance with this article, subject to a decision to be taken after 1 January 2017 by the same majority of States Parties as is required for the adoption of an amendment to the Statute.

4. A determination of an act of aggression by an organ outside the Court shall be without prejudice to the Court's own findings under this Statute.

5. This article is without prejudice to the provisions relating to the exercise of jurisdiction with respect to other crimes referred to in article 5.

5. The following text is inserted after article 25, paragraph 3, of the Statute:

3 *bis*. In respect of the crime of aggression, the provisions of this article shall apply only to persons in a position effectively to exercise control over or to direct the political or military action of a State.

6. The first sentence of article 9, paragraph 1, of the Statute is replaced by the following sentence:

1. 'Elements of Crimes shall assist the Court in the interpretation and application of articles 6, 7, 8 and 8 *bis*.

7. The chapeau of article 20, paragraph 3, of the Statute is replaced by the following paragraph; the rest of the paragraph remains unchanged:

3. No person who has been tried by another court for conduct also proscribed under article 6, 7, 8 or 8 *bis* shall be tried by the Court with respect to the same conduct unless the proceedings in the other court:

Annex II

Amendments to the Elements of Crimes

Article 8 *bis*
Crime of aggression

Introduction

1. It is understood that any of the acts referred to in article 8 *bis*, paragraph 2, qualify as an act of aggression.

2. There is no requirement to prove that the perpetrator has made a legal evaluation as to whether the use of armed force was inconsistent with the Charter of the United Nations.

3. The term "manifest" is an objective qualification.

4. There is no requirement to prove that the perpetrator has made a legal evaluation as to the "manifest" nature of the violation of the Charter of the United Nations.

Elements

1. The perpetrator planned, prepared, initiated or executed an act of aggression.

2. The perpetrator was a person[1] in a position effectively to exercise control over or to direct the political or military action of the State which committed the act of aggression.

3. The act of aggression – the use of armed force by a State against the sovereignty, territorial integrity or political independence of another State, or in any other manner inconsistent with the Charter of the United Nations – was committed.

4. The perpetrator was aware of the factual circumstances that established that such a use of armed force was inconsistent with the Charter of the United Nations.

5. The act of aggression, by its character, gravity and scale, constituted a manifest violation of the Charter of the United Nations.

6. The perpetrator was aware of the factual circumstances that established such a manifest violation of the Charter of the United Nations.

[1] With respect to an act of aggression, more than one person may be in a position that meets these criteria.

Annex III

Understandings regarding the amendments to the Rome Statute of the International Criminal Court on the Crime of Aggression

Referrals by the Security Council

1. It is understood that the Court may exercise jurisdiction on the basis of a Security Council referral in accordance with article 13, paragraph (b), of the Statute only with respect to crimes of aggression committed after a decision in accordance with article 15 *ter*, paragraph 3, is taken, and one year after the ratification or acceptance of the amendments by thirty States Parties, whichever is later.

2. It is understood that the Court shall exercise jurisdiction over the crime of aggression on the basis of a Security Council referral in accordance with article 13, paragraph (b), of the Statute irrespective of whether the State concerned has accepted the Court's jurisdiction in this regard.

Jurisdiction *ratione temporis*

3. It is understood that in case of article 13, paragraph (a) or (c), the Court may exercise its jurisdiction only with respect to crimes of aggression committed after a decision in accordance with article 15 *bis*, paragraph 3, is taken, and one year after the ratification or acceptance of the amendments by thirty States Parties, whichever is later.

Domestic jurisdiction over the crime of aggression

4. It is understood that the amendments that address the definition of the act of aggression and the crime of aggression do so for the purpose of this Statute only. The amendments shall, in accordance with article 10 of the Rome Statute, not be interpreted as limiting or prejudicing in any way existing or developing rules of international law for purposes other than this Statute.

5. It is understood that the amendments shall not be interpreted as creating the right or obligation to exercise domestic jurisdiction with respect to an act of aggression committed by another State.

Other understandings

6. It is understood that aggression is the most serious and dangerous form of the illegal use of force; and that a determination whether an act of aggression has been committed requires consideration of all the circumstances of each particular case, including the gravity of the acts concerned and their consequences, in accordance with the Charter of the United Nations.

7. It is understood that in establishing whether an act of aggression constitutes a manifest violation of the Charter of the United Nations, the three components of character, gravity and scale must be sufficient to justify a "manifest" determination. No one component can be significant enough to satisfy the manifest standard by itself.

End Notes

[1] Statement of David Scheffer, Ambassador at Large for War Crimes Issues, to the U.S. Senate Committee on Foreign Relations, July 23, 1998.

[2] 22 U.S.C. § 7421 et seq.

In: International Criminal Court
Editor: Michael N. Baker
ISBN: 978-1-61324-694-8

Chapter 5

STATEMENT OF HAROLD HONGJU KOH, LEGAL ADVISER, U.S. DEPARTMENT OF STATE AT THE REVIEW CONFERENCE OF THE INTERNATIONAL CRIMINAL COURT*

Kampala, Uganda
June 4, 2010

Thank you, Mr. Chairman

I am honored to present the views of the United States of America at this historic conference with respect to the proposed amendments to the Rome Statute, particularly the crime of aggression. We commend the Bureau, the Special Working Group on the Crime of Aggression, and all participating states—both parties and non-parties—as well as the many committed civil society organizations for all the hard work that has been done to bring us to this point.

As my colleague Ambassador Stephen Rapp noted earlier this week, the United States comes to this Conference in the spirit of renewed engagement,

* This is an edited, reformatted and augmented version of statement given by Harold Hongju Koh, Legal Adviser, The United States Department of State at the Review Conference of the International Criminal Court, on June 4, 2010.

with the aims of supporting a constructive outcome that is based on consensus, that strengthens the Court as an institution, and that advances the cause of human rights and international criminal justice. We are engaged in a complex exercise of making international criminal law for the real world. To be a success, this Review Conference must promote a principled, workable system of international criminal justice that is consistent with existing international law and institutions and fair both to victims of abuse and to individuals who may eventually be prosecuted for the crime of aggression. We cannot credibly claim success if we produce an unworkable and divisive compromise that weakens the Court, diverts it from its core human rights mission, or undermines our multilateral system of peace and security.

At the midpoint of this Review Conference, we can discern two points of genuine agreement among the delegates with regard to the proposed amendments. The first is that if any amendments to the Rome Statute are adopted, they should be adopted by consensus. The second is that there are several significant issues on which no consensus solution appears to be emerging.

The first question is what is the legitimate way to adopt amendments that add crimes to the Rome Statute? This is a bedrock procedural question that affects both the amendments regarding aggression and the Belgian amendment. We have heard states from every continent urge that any amendments regarding the crime of aggression be adopted by consensus. At the same time, we have heard disagreements over whether proposed amendments should be adopted under Article 121(4), Article 121(5), or some combination thereof. Further disagreements exist about the extent to which amendments under Article 121(5) apply to states that do not accept the amendments and non-state parties; and about whether states that do not accept the amendments are obligated to cooperate with the Court in cases involving nationals of accepting states. This lack of clarity about the amendment rule applies to the Belgian amendment as well, which we believe should also be adopted by genuine consensus. Under these circumstances, we can only conclude that, at this moment, proceeding by consensus is the only procedure that enjoys consensus support.

For something as fundamental to this Court as its core crimes, a rule of amendment by consensus is both necessary and appropriate. In the history of the International Criminal Court, the definitions of all of the crimes over which the Court has jurisdiction and all of the elements of these crimes have been adopted by consensus. We should not deviate from that decision-making principle for these even more sensitive and highly-charged offenses.

Proceeding by consensus is the soundest way to develop international law, and the best way to build a strong institution that can effectively improve the plight of victims. We cannot adopt amendments relating to a crime under conditions that ensure that every aggression prosecution will begin with a challenge to the legitimacy of the process by which the crime was adopted.

A second question is when should any aggression amendments enter into force and become operational? In listening to all of the statements, we have heard no consensus that it would be wise or desirable to operationalize the crime of aggression at this moment in the Court's development. Nor have we heard any consensus that the elements of the crime, which have been little discussed, should be completed here in Kampala. For the three existing crimes genocide, war crimes, and crimes against humanity the elements of the crimes were not finalized until nearly four years after Rome. Even if a definition of aggression were adopted, we would need a similar period of careful deliberation regarding the elements of what is a far less well-settled offense.

A third question is what jurisdictional conditions filters or triggers must be satisfied before the ICC could exercise jurisdiction over the crime of aggression? Although the Princeton Process addressed this issue at length, it was unable to bridge very significant differences of views among states on these issues. The Princeton Process did show support for the proposition that investigations and prosecutions for the crime of aggression could go forward where the Security Council had determined that aggression had occurred. But apart from that, there was little agreement regarding any filters or triggers beyond the Security Council. At the Resumed Session in New York, the views of states were categorized into four "Boxes," depending on whether states considered that there should be a requirement for a Security Council determination, and whether the consent of the involved states would be a prerequisite for exercising jurisdiction. We heard a number of states express preferences for Box 1 (Security Council filters); others for Box 3 (consent-based jurisdictional filters); and still others for Box 4 (no jurisdictional filter) solutions. Based on this striking diversity of views, we can only conclude that no consensus has emerged for a jurisdictional filter that could operationalize this crime, and that more work on this issue still needs to be done.

A fourth major question is whether, despite the considered attention that has been given to Article 8bis, genuine consensus has been reached regarding the meaning of the proposed definition of the crime of aggression? Here, we acknowledge that the Special Working Group was able to develop a definition, Article 8bis, on whose wording many nations agreed. Although we respect the considerable effort that has gone into the Princeton Process, we believe that without agreed-upon understandings, the current draft definition remains flawed. We are concerned that the apparent consensus on the wording of Article 8bis masks sharp disagreement on particular points regarding the meaning of that language that must be addressed before the amendments on the crime of aggression can enter into force.

In this regard, the two papers circulated by the Chair to help facilitate today's meeting—the Conference Room Paper and the Chairman's Non-paper—make a valuable contribution. They introduce the idea of addressing concerns through understandings or other documents, without the need for disturbing the language of Article 8bis itself. This is a constructive approach that we believe is worthy of further exploration and development. If the States Parties were to adopt the definition here in Kampala, we believe that understandings would be essential to minimize at least three undesirable risks.

First is the risk of criminalizing lawful uses of force. No one has ever before successfully prosecuted mere acts of aggression, as opposed to the "wars of aggression" that were prosecuted in Nuremberg and Tokyo. Many of the acts listed in Article 8bis might be elements of an illegal "war of aggression" the crime that was actually prosecuted at Nuremberg and that is discussed in Resolution 3314 but if committed in isolation, would not necessarily qualify as the crime of aggression. The current definition in Article 8bis does not fully acknowledge, as President Obama did in his recent Nobel acceptance speech, that certain uses of force remain both lawful and necessary. If Article 8bis were to be adopted as a definition, understandings would need to make clear that those who undertake efforts to prevent war crimes, crimes against humanity or genocide the very crimes that the Rome Statute is designed to deter do not commit "manifest" violations of the U.N. Charter within the meaning of Article 8bis. Regardless of how states may view the legality of such efforts, those who plan them are not committing the "crime of aggression" and should not run the risk of prosecution. At the same time, in order for an investigation or prosecution to proceed, it must be shown that it was manifest that the action was not undertaken in self-defense, without the consent of the state in question, and without any authorization provided by the Security Council.

A second risk is that adopting Article 8bis as the definition of aggression does not truly reflect customary international law, i.e., widespread and consistent state practice followed out of a sense of legal obligation. Although supporters of the Article 8bis definition claim that it mirrors the provisions of General Assembly Resolution 3314, in fact the text departs from that resolution in significant ways. Resolution 3314 states that only the most serious and dangerous forms of illegal uses of force constitute aggression, with the determination whether an act of aggression has occurred requiring careful consideration of the circumstances of each particular case, including the purpose for which force was used. Unlike genocide, war crimes, and crimes against humanity which plainly violated customary international law when the Rome Statute was adopted as yet, no authoritative definition of aggression exists under customary international law. If the Article 8bis language is not adapted to bring it into conformity with customary international law, it should be made clear that the language is being adopted only for purposes of implementing the Rome Statute and is not intended as an authoritative statement of customary international law. In any event, adopting the substance of a definition that might make sense as a General Assembly recommendation to a political body, such as the Security Council, does not necessarily make sense as a crime punishable by a judicial body. If the proposed definition were adopted, understandings should make clear that only the most serious and dangerous forms of illegal use of force constitute acts of aggression, and all relevant factors must be considered in each particular case to assess whether any particular use of force constitutes an act of aggression.

A third risk is that of unjustified domestic prosecutions. Too little attention has yet been paid to the question of how, if at all, the principle of complementarity would apply to the crime of aggression. The definition does little to limit the risk that State Parties will incorporate a definition particularly one we believe is flawed into their domestic law, encouraging the possibility that under expansive principles of jurisdiction, government officials will be prosecuted for alleged aggression in the courts of another state. Even if states incorporate an acceptable definition into their domestic law, it is not clear whether or when it is appropriate for one state to bring its neighbor's leaders before its domestic courts for the crime of aggression. Such domestic prosecutions would not be subject to any of the filters under consideration here, and would ask the domestic courts of one country to sit in judgment upon the state acts of other countries in a manner highly unlikely to promote peace and security.

In addition, any understandings must acknowledge that the question of how properly to define the crime of aggression is not logically independent from the issue of triggers and filters. The Princeton Process repeatedly reaffirmed that nothing is agreed until everything is agreed. If the issue of filters and triggers is decided separately from the definition itself, it should be clearly understood that the definition might need to be revisited upon future consideration of the filter and other related issues.

In sum, the first week of this Conference has revealed that there is no consensus on a number of contested issues such as the amendment rule and jurisdictional filters and triggers and that other issues such as the elements of the crime's definition simply cannot be resolved properly in the days remaining. Some of the other issues we have addressed particularly what understandings and conditions should be attached to the definition of the crime of aggression are discussed in preliminary form in the Conference Room Paper and the Chairman's Non-paper. We hope that the Conference can now turn urgently to develop these ideas and to see what consensus is genuinely possible in our time left here in Kampala.

In closing, let me reiterate: under the Obama Administration, the United States will continue to support institutions and prosecutions that hold accountable those who intentionally target innocent civilians. All of the members of our delegation have been deeply moved by testimony we have heard over the years, and especially during this week, from victims of war crimes. The United States is committed to taking concrete steps to ease the plight of those harmed by the crimes of greatest international concern. But this does not requiring imposing artificial deadlines on our important work. We should be determined to stay with the task long enough to ensure that we can accomplish something of enduring value to the people to whom we owe protection. Surely, finishing the unfinished business of Rome does not mean rushing to a premature conclusion on institution-transforming amendments on which there is not yet genuine consensus. Instead, finishing the work of Rome means building a stronger Court, with a renewed commitment to pursuing meaningful solutions by genuine consensus that can advance the cause of human rights and international justice.

Thank you.

In: International Criminal Court
Editor: Michael N. Baker

ISBN: 978-1-61324-694-8

Chapter 6

SPECIAL BRIEFING- HAROLD HONGJU KOH- LEGAL ADVISOR, U.S. DEPARTMENT OF STATE AND STEPHEN J. RAPP- AMBASSADOR-AT-LARGE FOR WAR CRIMES ISSUES*

U.S. ENGAGEMENT WITH THE INTERNATIONAL CRIMINAL COURT AND THE OUTCOME OF THE RECENTLY CONCLUDED REVIEW CONFERENCE

Washington, DC
June 15, 2010

MR. DUGUID: Good afternoon, ladies and gentlemen. Welcome to the State Department. We have a special briefing to lead off our daily press briefing today. Recently, there was an International Criminal Court conference in Kampala, Uganda. Our delegation was led by our Legal Advisor Dr. Harold

* This is an edited, reformatted and augmented version of Special Briefing given by Harold Hongju Koh- Legal Advisor, The United States Department of State, and by Stephen J. Rapp- Ambassador-At-Large for War Crimes Issues on The Unite States Engagement with the International Criminal Court and the Outcome of the Recently Concluded Review Conference, on June 15, 2010.

Koh and Ambassador-at-Large for War Crimes Issues Stephen Rapp. We have them both here today to take your questions and tell you a little bit about the achievements of the U.S. delegation at the conference.

We'll start with Professor Koh.

MR. KOH: Thanks, Gordon. We just returned from a two-week review conference of the International Criminal Court's Assembly of States Parties in Kampala, Uganda, which we attended as an observer nation.

Ambassador Rapp and I headed an interagency delegation that included representatives from State, Justice, Defense, the Uniformed Services, and the National Security Council. Our delegation worked extremely hard to resume engagement with the court, the states parties, observer nations, and many private organizations involved in international criminal justice. And we engaged in countless hours of conversation in plenary private meetings, et cetera.

The conference completed three main tasks. It endorsed and supported the court's core work with respect to the traditional crimes of genocide, war crimes, and crimes against humanity, and highlighted issues of state cooperation, peace and justice, stocktaking, and participation of victims, about which Ambassador Rapp will say more. It also adopted two new crimes, prohibition and non-international armed conflict of certain weapons, the so-called Belgian amendment, and a crime of aggression whose elements will be reconsidered and affirmatively considered after seven more years.

We think that with respect to the two new crimes, the outcome protected our vital interests. The court cannot exercise jurisdiction over the crime of aggression without a further decision to take place sometime after January 1st, 2017. The prosecutor cannot charge nationals of non-state parties, including U.S. nationals, with a crime of aggression. No U.S. national can be prosecuted for aggression so long as the U.S. remains a non-state party. And if we were to become a state party, we'd still have the option to opt out from having our nationals prosecuted for aggression. So we ensure total protection for our Armed Forces and other U.S. nationals going forward.

Under the terms of the resolution adopted, any crime of aggression couldn't become operational unless it were affirmatively adopted after another review by consensus or a two-thirds decision of all states parties no earlier than January 1, 2017. It could not be exercised except for acts committed one year after 30 states parties accepted the amendment. And two ways of referring to the crime would be created – one channel that would go through an exclusive Security Council trigger, and a second channel which would go through a prior Security Council review subject to four conditions.

If the Security Council did not make a determination that aggression had occurred, the prosecutor would have to offer a reasonable basis for investigating the crime under a definition that's been clarified by understandings we suggested. The prosecution would have to get a majority vote of six judges of the court's pretrial division. The Security Council would still, at that point, have the authority to stop the prosecution with a red light Chapter 7 resolution disapproving the resolution. And as I said, the channel would not apply to nationals of non-state parties or any non-consenting state party who opted out.

This issue has occupied the states parties and, in some sense, diverted the court from its core human rights mission. Many states and Kampala expressed an impulse to finalize the crime. Now, a non-final approach has been tentatively reached which takes the issue off the table for the next seven years with a notional solution that can be reexamined in 2017.

The United States considered the definition of aggression flawed, but a number of important safeguards were adopted. Understandings were adopted to make the definition more precise, to ensure that the crime will be applied only to the most egregious circumstances. And while we think the final resolution took insufficient account of the Security Council's assigned role to define aggression, the states parties rejected solutions that provided for jurisdiction without a Security Council or consent-based screen. We hope that crime will be improved in the future and will continue to engage toward that end.

The big picture going forward, I think we should keep in mind, is that as the country of Nuremberg prosecutor Justice Jackson, we are the only country that has successfully prosecuted the crime of aggression at Nuremberg and Tokyo. Of course, we do not commit aggression and the chances are extremely remote that a prosecution on this crime will, at some point in the distant future, affect us negatively.

So to paraphrase Churchill, this is not the end, it was not the beginning of the end, but it did feel like the end of the beginning of the U.S's 12-year relationship with this court. After 12 years, I think we have reset the default on the U.S. relationship with the court from hostility to positive engagement. In this case, principled engagement worked to protect our interest, to improve the outcome, and to bring us renewed international goodwill. As one delegate put it to me, the U.S. was once again seen, with respect to the ICC, as part of the solution and not the problem. The outcome in Kampala demonstrates again principled engagement can protect and advance our interests, it can help the states parties to find better solutions, and make for a better court, better protection of our interests, and a better relationship going forward between the U.S. and the ICC.

And let me turn it over to Ambassador Rapp.

AMBASSADOR RAPP: Well, thank you very much, Harold. I think one of the main aspects of this conference in which I think our principled engagement was so positive was working with the court in the stocktaking exercises, which looked at issues like complementarity, which is this idea that you should have justice at the national level in preference to justice at the international level. And that means strengthening national systems so that they can prosecute war crimes and genocide and crimes against humanity, the need for greater cooperation with this court, greater recognition of the rights and the concerns of victims and affected communities, and making sure that we proceed with the process of justice in a way that benefits the search for peace.

The sessions that went on the first week, we participated in very actively. We, ourselves, together with the Norwegian Government and the Government of the Democratic Republic of Congo, had a separate session on accountability in the DRC, which is, I think you all know, is a prime concern of Secretary Clinton with the enormous levels of atrocity that are ongoing there, the thousands of rapes that are committed every month. International justice alone, a few cases tried at The Hague, doesn't, even if there is full cooperation an arrest of each of the suspects, and there's still one at large doesn't have the kind of effect that you need to have on the ground if you're going to protect people from those crimes.

So we focused, in those sessions, on ways in which we as a donor state, and a very generous one, together with the EU and other partners, can strengthen justice on the ground. And that was a message that had a very receptive audience in Africa, where there is a strong desire to see these cases prosecuted in the national system, but with help in terms of capacity and independence to ensure that justice is done. This whole conference, I think, gave us an opportunity to engage with the ICC and work toward making this institution more effective.

The United States, as everyone knows, has been a leader in international justice, beginning with Nuremberg, that Harold mentioned, and in Tokyo, but particularly beginning, again, in 1993 with the establishment of the Yugoslavia Court, the following year with the establishment of the International Criminal Tribunal for Rwanda where I worked, and thereafter with the Special Court for

Sierra Leone and other international institutions where we were a large contributor to those courts, in which Americans played leadership roles, and in which, beyond even our formal role, we provided assistance to those courts and information sharing and witness protection and diplomatic support, and support and efforts to arrest suspects. And even while we don't become a member of the ICC, the opportunity to do some of those same kinds of things presents itself with the ICC, where that court is pursuing the same kind of cases that we prosecuted through these international institutions in Rwanda and Sierra Leone.

We've had a concern in the past that the prosecutor of the ICC could make could undertake politically motivated prosecutions, could perhaps come after Americans who were engaged in protecting people from atrocity instead of emphasizing those that were committing the crimes. Thus far, this court has been appropriately focused. The cases that it has taken up in Northern Uganda involving Joseph Kony and the crimes of the Lord's Resistance Army in the DRC, the various militia groups that have engaged in campaigns of mass atrocity in Darfur, Sudan, and in the Central African Republic were cases that cried out for justice and accountability and for the protection of the victims.

And if it weren't for the ICC, the UN would have been having to go in and establish a special court for those kinds of situations. So as we recognized in March when we participated in the Assembly of States Parties in New York, it's in our interest to support those prosecutions not at this time as a member of the ICC, but in kind with assistance as long as it's consistent with our law. And at the same time that we support those prosecutions, also work on the whole of the international justice system, the key part of which is that that is below the level of the international system, the massive amount of work that needs to be done at the national level. That message of our commitment and our support for appropriate prosecutions at this court, I think, resonated very well when we came to this issue of aggression, where those of us that have worked in international justice know how challenging it is to prosecute, to arrest, to obtain cooperation. Even when you're going after the cases that involve mass atrocity, people accuse you of being politically motivated.

But what's happened, as we've seen in the last 15 years, is that when a leader has been charged by one of these courts, and there's strong evidence of his involvement in mass atrocity against innocent civilians, eventually it becomes possible to dislodge that leader, as we saw with Milosevic and as we saw with Charles Taylor, and bring that person to justice. If the court, on the other hand, were to get into the political area and to deal with crimes not against individual civilians, as in war crimes or crimes against humanity or genocide, but crimes against states and the crime of aggression, it would find it even more difficult to obtain cooperation, and it would quickly find itself by haven taken one side or another, even accepted a case or rejected a case involving a border conflict, really stymied from the point of view of getting the kind of cooperation that it needs to deal with atrocity crimes.

And that was an argument that resonated very strongly, and 50 human rights organizations across the world agreed with us on that point and put out a letter to the foreign ministers of the ICC countries, saying it wasn't a good idea for this court to go there. What happened is, as Harold said, in the end is that we had a deferral, at least, of the ability of this court to move into the aggression area until 2017. Even then, it'll take a vote comparable to the vote we would have had in Kampala; a vote by an overwhelming majority or a consensus in favor of going forward. This gives the court seven more years to get it right in terms of going after atrocity crime.

As I think everyone knows, the Yugoslavia and Rwanda tribunals, even though they've not moved as quickly as some would have liked, and these cases have sometimes been difficult, the results show that almost 200 people have been prosecuted, including chiefs of state and heads of government and immediate leaders like those I prosecuted in Rwanda and others. Thus far, the ICC has only begun two trials and hasn't concluded them. And this court has a ways to go before it's as effective as the ad hoc tribunals were. This next seven years gives them an opportunity, I think, to be effective, and to the extent consistent with our law, at least in the situations that have been open so far, we're prepared to do what we can to assist those prosecutions to ensure that these crimes that shock the universal conscience result in accountability for those that bear the greatest responsibility.

So with that opening, I guess we can go to questions.

MR. DUGUID: Yes. Please, as you ask your question, direct it to either Professor Koh or Ambassador Rapp, Matt, and then okay.

QUESTION: Yeah. Well, actually, this is for both of you. I guess I'm not exactly sure what you guys spent two weeks doing except for thwarting the idea basically making sure that something that they wanted to do didn't happen and has been pushed down the road till 2017, and even then, it's going to take there are so many conditions attached to this that it probably it sounds as though it's almost impossible for it will be almost impossible for the court to take up the crime of aggression. I'm wondering, what were you worried about? If you hadn't gone and engaged, did you think that they would have actually agreed on this and to start prosecuting this crime immediately?

And then second of all, you talked about how you've reset the default from hostility to engagement, but in fact, the Bush Administration was cooperated in several notable instances, cases that the LRA and in Darfur. So how exactly is this Administration different than the last one?

MR. KOH: Matt, we didn't thwart anything. We worked with the other countries who were there to reach a consensus outcome, which was reached. The first week was entirely about the core mission of the court genocide, war crimes, and crimes against humanity. We made presentations there; we participated in discussions about a set of issues going to ensuring successful prosecutions.

The International Criminal Court has not completed a case. And that's an important fact. The aggression issue is a second agenda. One prosecutor there said to me the challenge is how do you land on Mars when you haven't proved you can land on the moon? So the first week was all about strengthening the core agenda of the court. The second week was about trying to decide what kind of consensus outcome there could be with regard to the crime of aggression. And there were many different views on the table. I think everybody realized that more time was needed. And the consensus outcome, which was achieved on the last day was what I described, adopting a non-final outcome to be reconsidered. But seven years from now, the court may be quite advanced in other respects as a stronger institution with the development of U.S. engagement.

Now, you say that this was the strategy or policy of a previous administration. The fact of the matter is that in the early days, there was hostility to the court getting sufficient membership. There are now 111 states parties. It's not going to go away. The only approach that we think ensures our interests and ensure that the court accomplishes its core mission is a strategy of engagement. And so we think that after 12 years of back and forth on different approaches, that will be the default, and we think it's one that serves our interests and makes for a stronger court.

AMBASSADOR RAPP: I should note that, I mean, a number of resolutions were passed high-level ministerial statement on cooperation and on mechanisms for increasing coordination between donors when it comes to strengthening the national justice systems. And so there were, I think, constructive steps taken by the court. And the cooperation indeed was also requested, as we suggested, of non-party states like ourselves. Because when I was in the Sierra Leone court, we sought assistance of states that weren't obliged to assist us, and they did. And so it's important that that occur.

On this whole question of engagement and what we accomplished, what we saw when this Administration took over in 2009 and was that there had been this process of studying the crime of aggression for the last six or seven years a working group that actually met in Princeton, New Jersey and that came up with recommendations about how to proceed. And it reached a consensus outcome on defining the crime of aggression. Everyone seemed to think the definition was very good. We thought it very vague, a definition that would allow a court to be involved in any so-called manifest violation, without really defining what that was that could have gotten the court into border disputes, could have involved in it prosecuting people, or going in to protect civilians as we did in Kosovo from atrocities, from war crimes and crimes against humanity.

And because we weren't present, some things ended up in that process that I think probably wouldn't have been there if we'd been involved. We had to play catch-up with that. And as Harold said, we were successful in adding several understandings to that definition. Those understandings wouldn't have been there were it not for our participation that ensured that this court would not deal with but any of the most serious cases, that there would have to be not just character, gravity, or scale, but a combination of several of those factors, and that this wouldn't lead to national prosecutions of leaders for aggression by alleged aggression by other states.

So I think it was successful because we raised issues, raised questions, not in a negative sort of way, but just simply said, "What about this, what about this, what about this?" And through our engagement, I think we accomplished quite a lot. We also raised this issue about the court needing, really, to become a bicycle. As Harold used the example, at the moment, it's just starting out and it's a bit wobbly; let's not overload it with this thing. And so the result was basically a deferral of this issue for seven years. But significantly, provisions have gone into the statute that can't be changed in 2017 by this process, which will protect the nationals of non-party states like ourselves, or states that opt out. So and I don't think that would have occurred were it not for us sort of raising the issues in this conference.

But in all of the engagement that we had, we found states from each continent that considered our concerns very carefully, and worked to accommodate those concerns. And indeed, in the process of discussion, other concerns were raised by individual parties. And I think as a result, the process was much better and the result was much better, not just for the United States, but for this court itself.

MR. DUGUID: Thank you. Charlie and then Elise.

QUESTION: For Professor Koh, I'm intrigued by your use of the word "reset," because, not surprisingly, at least to me, it has a more of a political tinge on the diplomatic – in the diplomatic dictionary in this Administration. And obviously, I don't think you used the word just out of the out of thin air. And maybe I'm missing something. Is there a legal part to it as well? Or was, in fact, the main purpose of going to the conference, attending the way you did, to make things right or get on the other side with the ICC in a political sense?

MR. KOH: Well, Charlie, there are really three policies at work. One is our support for policies of accountability, international criminal justice, and ending impunity, which lead to our supporting international criminal tribunals ad hoc, of the kind – Rwanda, Yugoslavia, Sierra Leone, Cambodia, et cetera.

A second policy is a policy of principled engagement with existing international institutions, whether it be the Human Rights Council, the Copenhagen process, the nuclear security process. And then the third point, which was illustrated by President Obama's Nobel lecture, is that in the 21st century, sometimes there are uses of force in which nations must engage that are lawful. And the question is how to make sure that they are not criminalized if they are lawful.

Now, I think one fundamental point is that the crime of aggression is different from the other three crimes in a couple of respects. As Steve pointed out, there have been hundreds of prosecutions for genocide, war crimes, and crimes against humanity. There have only been two prosecutions for wars of aggression, namely Nuremberg and Tokyo. Both of those happened before there was a UN system. There's been no successful prosecution for an act of aggression alone. And the question is, since we're making international criminal law for the real world, before you lock in the crime forever, you want to make sure that as a legal matter you've got it right.

And a lot of our focus on this was clarifying, as lawyers do, what terms mean, to make sure that it deters to the appropriate extent but doesn't over or under-deter; to talk exactly about what the jurisdictional filters and trigger mechanisms were going to be; and I think most important, to reaffirm the principle that when you have an organic change in an institution like this, it should be done on a consensus basis.

The other three crimes were adopted by consensus approaches at Rome. And we thought it was very important that if you're going to add to the criminal array available to this court, it should also be done by unanimity of view by the interested parties.

MR. DUGUID: Thank you. Elise.

QUESTION: Yes. For either one of you, maybe both hi.

AMBASSADOR RAPP: How are you doing?

QUESTION: Nice to see you.

I'm just wondering what the end game is here with this Administration and the court. Are you trying to shape the court in a way that, ultimately, you can perhaps consider becoming a signatory to the court? Or are you just concerned necessarily about other crimes that you see and the way that they should be prosecuted to make sure that international justice is upheld?

Because I just I do it is kind of curious that an administration would become so engaged in shaping the kind of format of a court that it's not a signatory to. And what gives us the moral authority to do that if we're not becoming a signatory to the court? And in addition, are you conditioning any kind of future U.S. assistance with the court on some of the objectives that you proposed at the conference?

MR. KOH: Well, first of all, the other countries all wanted us to engage. Their recognition, as a historical matter, as international institutions and courts with which the United States is not involved tend not to be as effective. Secondly, they noticed that all of the ad hoc tribunals – the Yugoslav and Rwanda tribunal, the Cambodia tribunal – have been more successful by virtue of deep U.S. engagement.

Third, the other strategies that have been used, either isolation from the court or hostility from the court, appear to be non-starters. You have now a court that exists, it's functioning, it's hearing cases, and needs help. And it needs people who are both going to criticize things that it does that are less well thought through and to try to suggest directions in which it can go.

I don't think we're talking so much about an end game as we are talking about a process, the default

QUESTION: A process by which eventually you hope that you can join?

MR. KOH: I think our basic conviction is a strategy of engagement is good for the court and good for U.S. interests. We might as well start that process and make a serious effort at it, which is what we did. And as I said, the reaction was favorable. On the last day, they said, "We're delighted to see a situation in which the U.S. is part of the solution for the court and not part of the problem."

AMBASSADOR RAPP: I mean, it's clear that joining the court is not on the table, as far as a U.S. decision at this time. But as you know, the United States takes a very long time to adopt international conventions and treaties, and sometimes doesn't. I mean, it took us 40 years to ratify the Genocide Convention.

I think what we're looking at here is how this court develops. We want to see it develop responsibly, to focus on crimes that involve truly massive intentional attacks on civilians, both in terms of the decisions made by its prosecutor on where to open investigations and also by its chambers, its trial chambers that have to decide whether, sometimes, to authorize those investigations or to issue arrest warrants.

And I think over time, there's a possibility that we may gain confidence in this institution and that would enable us to move forward. And who knows what the future may hold? But at this time, we recognize that this institution is the international court where justice will be delivered if it can't be delivered at the national or the regional level, that the United Nations is not going to step up and establish a Rwanda or Yugoslavia court and spend a hundred million or more a year on a court, as they have with those, when 111 countries are dues-paying members to this one.

And so this is where accountability is to be delivered. It's also recognized, as we've seen with Darfur, that the UN Security Council, of which we're a permanent member, has the ability to send cases to it involving not just the 111 countries but all 192. And so it's a tool in the international toolbox, so to speak, for achieving accountability instead of establishing a separate, one-off institution.

So, if for nothing else, because of that role, but also because we're so committed to achieving accountability for these cases and fulfilling the promise that we've made to victims when we went and convicted Jean Kambanda, the prime minister of Rwanda, for genocide, or brought Milosevic to trial or Charles Taylor to trial, there's been an expectation created that when people of whatever level commit mass atrocities against the innocent, there's going to be accountability. And we think that's appropriate. We want it done. We want it done fairly. We want it done effectively. And the ICC wants us to assist and to the extent it's consistent with our law and we do have some laws that we have to be careful about observing that are a little different in this area than they are with other courts. We want to go forward on this, and that's something that we'll be doing in the next several years and perhaps that will build an engagement and a confidence that will allow us to go further.

MR. DUGUID: Thank you. I believe we have time for one more question. Farah, please.

QUESTION: I was hoping you could tell us a little bit more about the discussions surrounding Sudan and the effectiveness – I mean, a lot of people watched with dismay and don't feel like the court has been positive – has gotten positive outcomes for people there. And I was hoping you could tell us a little bit more about the discussions there.

And my second question is about – you've talked a lot about strengthening national justice systems, and there's an awful lot of people who say, okay, the ICTR is the last time we're ever going to have the international community coming in and imposing a – sort of creating a justice system for a country, and more like they believe that we're going to see more like Sierra Leone and Cambodia, which is just assisting a national – I mean, do you feel that that's the future, or do you think that, in fact, there will be – the future really is in these international efforts?

AMBASSADOR RAPP: Well, first of all, on the Sudan issue and Kampala it was a good thing that this conference was in Africa and 30 countries in Africa more than I think there are about 55 countries in Africa but a substantial majority are members of the ICC. Uganda itself sent the first case to the ICC, the Kony case, by referral. And there were discussions, particularly in this Peace and Justice Forum, about the interplay of peace and justice, and the Sudan issue was there. But I think the bottom line of the conference is that everyone recognized that when there are cases before the court, states need to cooperate. And I think it strengthened the commitment of the African parties to assist in the cases in Africa and assisted the other countries in their resolve to ensure that arrests are made. So I think it actually was helpful to this challenging aspect of getting cooperation in Sudan.

In regard to the future of international justice, the possibility of ad hoc mixed courts at the national level I mean, the Sierra Leone is an example of that, though more international than national but where national judges sit with international judges, where there's international assistance to those courts, I think that remains very much an open possibility in the future. The ICC is never going to be able to prosecute more than three or four cases in each situation, and that and there may be situations where it's better to have a court close to the people, as we had in Sierra Leone or you have in Cambodia, with international help and assistance to provide the capacity and the independence, rather than send those cases thousands of miles away to The Hague.

And that's consistent with complementarity, consistent with the idea that it's better to do it at the national level. So I think our American interest will be to look for alternatives close to the ground, as we did in Kenya for instance, where we very strongly supported the Waki Commission report and the initiative of former Secretary General Annan that urged there to be a national independent court to deal with the post-election violence and to provide, perhaps, an international prosecutor in that or other international personnel to ensure the independence to give assurance to the victims that they wouldn't that they'd be properly treated because of some of the ethnic aspects of that conflict.

That's the best approach. Sadly, it didn't happen there. Because it didn't happen, it's gone to the ICC. But I think we'll always be working to try to do it there. And that was part of the message of the sessions on complementarity. There needs to be a continuum from the national level to the international, with the international level only handling a relative handful of cases and hopefully providing an incentive for countries to do it themselves so that it happens at the local level with their own people with assistance rather than thousands of miles administered by people that are unfamiliar with their culture and country.

MR. DUGUID: Thank you, Ambassador Rapp. Thank you, Professor Koh. Thank you for joining us, ladies and gentlemen. We'll begin with the daily press briefing shortly. That's all the time we have.

INDEX

B

C

F

G

H

I

J

K

L

M

N

O

P

T

U

V

W

Y

Z